Firstfruits and Harvest

Insights into Revelation, Book 3

Other Books by the Author

The Coming End of the Age

An Overview of the Endtime

Preparing For the Lord's Return

Greapa

The Coming of the King in Matthew 24 and 25

The Goal and Peak of Our Christian Experience
Insights into Revelation, Book 1

The Beast, His Image, and His Mark
Insights into Revelation, Book 2

A Place Prepared
Insights into Revelation, Book 4

The Church in Philadelphia
Insights into Revelation, Book 5

Delusion and God's Salvation

A Faithful God

Booklets by the Author

The Heart of God	The Rapture
The Heart of God II	Urgency or Complacency
The Heart of God III	A New Creation
The Heart of God IV	The Spirit
The Heart of God V	The Spirit Was Not Yet
The Heart of God VI	The Lark Ascending
Redemption and Salvation	The Order of Melchizedek
Signs of the End	The Prayer of the End

Visit **aplaceinthewilderness.com** for more about these books (including their introduction, table of contents, and ordering information) and booklets.

Firstfruits and Harvest

Insights into Revelation, Book 3

Paul Cozza

A Place in the Wilderness

Firstfruits and Harvest
Insights into Revelation, Book 3

© 2019 Paul Cozza

ISBN 978-1-5136-4035-8

All rights reserved.
No part of this publication may be reproduced or transmitted in any form or by any means — electronic, mechanical, or any other, including photocopy, recording, or any information or retrieval system — without prior written consent, in hardcopy paper form, from:

Paul Cozza
A Place in the Wilderness

Website: aplaceinthewilderness.com
Email: paul@aplaceinthewilderness.com

Second printing: July, 2025

Scripture quotations are from the American Standard Version of the Bible (1901) unless otherwise noted.

Cover picture from an original painting by Walter Waller Caffyn, RA

Cover design: Nuggitz Creative Services (Nuggitz.com)

Table of Contents

Preface 1
Introduction 3
   Type and Antitype 3
   Deficient Doctrines 4
   An Overview 5

Chapter 1 – Maturity 9
   A Matter of Life 9
   God's Desire 10
   The Flowing God 10
   Man's Cooperation 11
   Only a Few 12
   Awaiting Resurrection 14
   The Harvest 15
   Watch! 16
   Not Prevailing 16
   In Summary 17

Chapter 2 – The Time 19
   A Hidden Gathering 20
   The Moment 21
   Those Who Remain 23
   As a Thief 25
   In Summary 26

Chapter 3 – The Place 29
   The Throne of God 29
   The Eternal State 30
   The Righteous Judge 32
   Transcendent 33

- A Change of Realm 33
- To the Air 33
- A Change of Physical Position 35
- The Lord's Wisdom 35
- The Sea of Glass 36
- In Summary 37

Chapter 4 – The Means 39
- Taken 40
- Leaning upon the Beloved 40
- The Power of His Person 41
- The Out-Resurrection 42
- The Reality 43
- Left 45
- The Harvesters 47
- Caught Up, Caught Away 49
- In Summary 50

Chapter 5 – The State of Being 53
- The Great Voice 53
- The Wonderful Christ 54
- The Peak and Goal 58
- In Our Image 60
- Dried Out 60
- The Judgment Seat 62
- In Summary 63

Chapter 6 – The Eternal State 65
- Not As Thought 65
- A Person 66
- A Change of State 68
- Every One 69
- The Path of the Firstfruits 69

Remedial Action 70
The Spiritual Body 72
Punishment After Resurrection 73
Our True Nature Revealed 74
Our True Condition 75
The Need for Further Perfecting 77
Maimed, Halt, Blind 77
Adjusted in the Wedding Feast 79
Eternal Tabernacles 80
In Summary 82

Appendix – The Manchild 85
Not Forgotten 85

Bibliography 89

Note to the reader
Explanations and further details about portions of the text appear as footnotes at page bottoms. Verse references appear in the numbered **References** list at the end of each chapter.

Preface

Heaven and earth shall pass away, but my words shall not pass away. (Matt. 24:35)

But he answered and said, It is written, Man shall not live by bread alone, but by every word that proceedeth out of the mouth of God. (Matt. 4:4)

    God's speaking is eternal. What He says is truth; it never passes away or changes. The Lord Himself told us exactly this in Matthew 24. Man's speaking is temporal, fleeting, spoken today and forever gone tomorrow. But this is not so with God's speaking. The eternal Being speaks the eternal words.

    Every single word that comes forth from God's mouth is rich and life-giving. What kind of being is our God, that every single word is of enormous importance, filled with meaning and life? There is simply no one like Him and nothing like His speaking.

    And so, we come to this book. It centers on a single word, a seemingly innocuous pronoun in the book of Revelation. I cannot say how many times I took no notice of it. But that little word is also God's speaking.

    One day while I was reading the book of Revelation, that pronoun bothered me. It stood out; it didn't fit; it did not agree with my concept of the endtime, the rapture, and God's move on the earth. It just bothered me.

    Such is the word of God. It does not change and it won't go away. It *will* redo our concepts. As we take it in, and "chew" on it, it slowly changes us. It changes our minds and our hearts to gradually remake us into the image of Christ.

    This was my experience with this little pronoun. I had to wrestle with it, struggle with it, chew on it. It was like a piece of tough jerky to me. This wasn't because of the word itself, but because of my concepts and inadequate understanding. However, as I tossed this word to and fro, as I examined it first from one side and then another, slowly the door opened into something new, something I had not seen before, something full of light, and rich in meaning.

And so that single word led into this book. This is how the word of God is — a single word can open into the entire spiritual realm. Every single word of God is rich beyond measure, even the seemingly innocuous pronouns!

Introduction

And I saw, and behold, the Lamb standing on the mount Zion, and with him a hundred and forty and four thousand, having his name, and the name of his Father, written on their foreheads.... These were purchased from among men, to be the firstfruits unto God and unto the Lamb. (Rev. 14:1, 4)

And I saw, and behold, a white cloud; and on the cloud I saw one sitting like unto a son of man, having on his head a golden crown, and in his hand a sharp sickle. And another angel came out from the temple, crying with a great voice to him that sat on the cloud, Send forth thy sickle, and reap: for the hour to reap is come; for the harvest of the earth is ripe. And he that sat on the cloud cast his sickle upon the earth; and the earth was reaped. (Rev. 14:14-16)

Revelation 14 is an overview of the last years of this age. It begins with a depiction of 144,000 firstfruits[*] standing with the Lamb before the throne of God on the heavenly Mount Zion. It moves on to the angelic warning given to mankind of God's impending judgment, which should refer to the judgment of the seventh seal with the seven trumpets. It then proceeds to the fall of Babylon the great. It next warns against worshipping the Antichrist and his image. It concludes with two harvests: the first, that of the believers; the second, that of the armies of the nations at Armageddon. The firstfruits and the harvest of the believers are the focus of this book.

Type and Antitype

Revelation is a harvest of all the seeds that were sown and have grown throughout the entire Bible. For example, in Genesis

---

[*] Actually, these 144,000 are not the only firstfruits – there are many more. See the book *The Goal and Peak of Our Christian Experience* for a detailed explanation of who comprises the firstfruits.

1-2 there are a man, a bride, the tree of life, a flowing river, gold, bdellium (a pearl-like resin), and precious stone (onyx). At the very end of the Bible, in Revelation 21-22, there are the Lamb, His bride (the new Jerusalem), the tree of life, the river of water of life, gold, pearl, and precious stones. What was sown in the first two chapters of the Bible is reaped in its final chapters. What began in the Old Testament consummates in Revelation.

In the Old Testament there are also firstfruits and harvest. These are types of the reality depicted in Revelation 14, which is the reaping of the seeds sown in Old Testament.

In the Old Testament the wheat-growing season was marked by two events. The first was the feast of harvest,[1] which was celebrated at the beginning of the season when the firstfruits of the harvest ripened. These were reaped from the fields and brought into God's house[2] as an offering to God.

The second was the feast of ingathering.[3] This occurred at the end of the year when the grain in the fields was fully ripened. This grain was not brought into God's house. Rather, it was for the people as the fruit of their labors.

As there were significant differences in these Old Testament types, so there will be in the reality of these types, when the Lord fully reaps His harvest at the end of this age. These differences will be explored in detail in this book.

Deficient Doctrines

There are various doctrines concerning the rapture. Most of them fall short of the truth, because they regard only part of what is revealed in the Bible. For example, one doctrine focuses on 1 Thessalonians, where it says that the living believers with the resurrected dead believers will be caught up to meet with the Lord in the air.[4] This verse, taken in conjunction with the verses in Matthew that seem to indicate that the believers will be taken before the great tribulation,[5] results in the doctrine called "pre-tribulation rapture." In this line of thought, all the believers are taken before the great endtime troubles strike earth.

Another doctrine of the rapture focuses on 1 Thessalonians and 1 Corinthians.[6] 1 Corinthians indicates that the rapture of the believers will occur at the last or seventh trumpet, which happens at the end of the tribulation. So, in this line of thought, all the believers are taken, but they are taken at the end of the tribulation. This is called "post-tribulation rapture."

These doctrines are partly right and partly in error. The difficulty with both of them is they focus on certain verses and overlook others that contradict the doctrine being propounded. In this book we will examine all the pertinent verses regarding the rapture of the believers, to gain a full understanding of the various aspects of that event.

Most doctrines regarding the rapture, and in fact most doctrines in general, are far too simplistic. They attempt to force real-life spiritual realities and physical happenings into the restrictive box of narrow thought. The consideration is that something must be this way or that. There is rarely the realization that both ways could be true and perhaps even more.

Regarding the Lord's great endtime harvest, there are actually quite a few aspects. For example, there are the gathering of the firstfruits, the rapture of the manchild, the resurrection and gathering of the Jewish overcomers, and the harvest of the main body of Christians including the resurrection of the dead believers. Furthermore, within these are various additional aspects.

We must not think that the endtime will be so simple. Consider how complicated are the earth, man, and each and every person. Dealing with each of these, and the complicated condition of each, is not simple. It requires God's working in many, varied aspects.

In addition, the doctrines regarding the rapture of the believers generally overlook one crucial aspect of that event – maturity in the divine life. Actually, regarding the rapture, the divine life is more than crucial. As we shall see, it is *vital*.

An Overview

This book focuses on two major aspects of the believers' rapture – the firstfruits and the harvest. Chapter 1 deals with the constituents of these two groups of believers. Who comprises the firstfruits and who the harvest? This chapter sets forth the matter of life as it relates to the rapture.

Chapter 2 looks at the time of the rapture – that is, when will the believers be taken from the earth. The verses concerning the timing of the rapture are examined in detail and properly placed for an accurate understanding of God's endtime harvest. Regarding the timing of the raptures of the firstfruits and the harvest, the Bible tells us very little for one, but quite much for the other.

Chapter 3 examines the place of the rapture. This does not refer to the place *from* which the believers are taken, but rather the place *to* which they are raptured. As we shall see, there is a very significant difference between the firstfruits and the harvest. In the Old Testament, type one was offered to God in His house, while the other was for the people.

Chapter 4 speaks about the means or the method of the rapture. It may come as a surprise, but the means by which the firstfruits and the harvest are gathered is not the same. This has seemingly been entirely overlooked. However, there is something quite significant hidden in God's word regarding it.

Chapter 5 discusses the spiritual condition of the believers when they are raptured. That is, in what state of being are the believers when they are taken from the earth. Again, these are not the same for the firstfruits and harvest. There is something very different about the firstfruits.

Finally, Chapter 6 looks into the eternal state of the believers. This is important in order to put into context the rapture of the believers at the endtime, their condition, and their portion during the millennium. Eventually, we all will arrive at the eternal state; however, our paths will differ greatly.

However, in writing this book I realized something must be said regarding the dear martyrs who throughout the centuries have laid down their lives for the Lord they loved. Therefore, the appendix details the very special case of the manchild in Revelation 12.

It is my sincere hope that at least some who read this book will be encouraged to seek after the Lord, grow in Him, and arrive at that to which we all have been called. May this book touch your heart and your mind, and lead you closer to our dear Lord Jesus.

References

[1] Ex. 23:16
[2] Ex. 23:19
[3] Ex. 23:16
[4] 1 Thes. 4:17
[5] Matt. 24:37-41
[6] 1 Cor. 15:51-52

8 Firstfruits and Harvest

CHAPTER 1

Maturity

Many Christians have the understanding that the rapture is simply an objective event that happens to all believers. They think that at some point in time God will simply transport the Christians to the heavens or to the air to be with the Lord Jesus. This understanding is inadequate. While on one level it is partly true, it ignores the vital role that the believers' growth in the divine life plays in the rapture.

A Matter of Life

Let both grow together until the harvest... (Matt. 13:30)

...as newborn babes, long for the spiritual milk which is without guile, that ye may grow thereby unto salvation... (1 Pet. 2:2)

...but speaking truth in love, may grow up in all things into him, who is the head, even Christ... (Eph. 4:15)

When Christ, who is our life, shall be manifested, then shall ye also with him be manifested in glory. (Col. 3:4)

Growth, growth, growth! The Christian life is one of growth. It begins with our rebirth, in which our human spirit is born of the divine Spirit.[1] At that time Christ is deposited into our spirit as the divine life,[2] and from that point in time He begins to grow within us. This is our regeneration.

As He grows He spreads within us from our spirit to our soul. Slowly, over a long period of time, our very person changes into His likeness. We are transformed from what we were into who He is, bit by bit, from glory to glory by the operation of the divine Spirit within us.[3] This is called transformation.

When the process is complete, when we are fully transformed into His image, then there is but one part of us that remains to be changed – our physical body. At the moment of the Father's choosing, the Christ who is within us as our life will burst forth and be manifested. This will change our physical bodies to be like His body.[4] This is called transfiguration. It was exhibited by the Lord on the mount of transfiguration,[5] and is a crucial part of what is called the rapture – the rapture that brings one to be with Christ at the throne of God.[6] There is another event that in some ways is similar to this, and it is also called the rapture. But it is *not* due to the growth and maturity of the divine life. This, of course, can lead to much confusion.

In this book the completed process of the divine life is seen in the firstfruits. The harvest of the main body of the believers, as we shall see, is of a different sort. In both instances believers are removed from the earth. However, there are differences between them in their character and in the time, place, and means of their rapture.

God's Desire

It is God's desire that all believers ripen and be taken from the earth before the time of trial comes during the last three and a half years of this age. And, all believers are given this possibility. All believers have access to Christ; all have access to the same one Spirit; all can enjoy Christ, gain Him, and become one with Him; all can grow and mature in Christ. Every Christian has the opportunity to fully mature in the Lord. However, not all Christians avail themselves of this.

The firstfruits ripen first and, in a sense, are special because of this. However, they are not special in life or nature. Every Christian shares God's divine life and divine nature. Nor are the firstfruits loved by God more than He loves other Christians. They are not treated in a special way by Him, for God is not a respecter of persons. He treats all of His children the same. He loves them all equally. What then causes the firstfruits to ripen first?

The Flowing God

And he showed me a river of water of life, bright as crystal, proceeding out of the throne of God and of the Lamb... (Rev. 22:1)

The growth in life of the believers is two-sided. From God's side there is the need for His life to flow out, that the believers might partake of and enjoy it daily, that they might grow in it. This outflowing of God's life is seen in the river of water of life flowing in the New Jerusalem. This river is a picture of God's abundant Spirit of life flowed out to man for his enjoyment. This river began in Genesis in the garden of Eden.[7] It continued to flow throughout the Old Testament in the Psalms[8] and in Ezekiel.[9] When the Lord came to the earth, He spoke of this flowing river as the wonderful gift of supply to those who believe into Him.[10] Eventually, God flows out eternally as the river of water of life in the New Jerusalem. No one can arrest God's flow!

God's life is also seen in the tree of life,[11] which is a picture of Christ as the food supply to God's people. Christ is the true vine,[12] the heavenly manna,[13] and the Passover sacrificed for us.[14] He is our spiritual food in many ways and of various kinds.

There is no problem with God in His pouring Himself out to man. He is a mighty flowing out, and has flowed throughout the ages. He was flowing in Genesis and will still flow out in Revelation. Throughout all time Satan has sought to stop God's flow, but he could not. No one can stop God's flowing! It spreads to reach everyone who is thirsty. Let him who is athirst drink freely of the water of life![15]

Man's Cooperation

God is an unstoppable flow; there is no problem from His side with respect to our growth in the divine life. However, there could be, and very frequently are, numerous problems from ours. Some of these are extremely serious. For example, we may not seek the Lord as we should; we may have no heart for Him. We may seek something else such as personal fame or fortune. We may not give ourselves to the Lord as we should; we may give ourselves to the world, to the flesh, to religion, or to something else other than God.

We may have problems within that hinder our growth in Christ, problems such as an overactive mind, wild emotions, a temper, stubbornness, contentiousness, pride, fantasies, delusions, and so many other internal obstructions. Any one of these can not only frustrate the growth of the divine life within, but stunt it. There are a seemingly unlimited number of things that can hinder the operation of the divine life. Any and all of these can lead us astray from that narrow path that leads to life.[16]

The firstfruits, however, cooperate entirely with God and with God's move in life within them. They give up the world — they are not part of it, nor do they love it.[17] They give up their past, letting go of all things that are behind.[18] They don't muse on their past, linger in it, or desire to return to it. They give up themselves. They hate their self,[19] that old man who has been crucified with Christ,[20] and they live according to that reality. When something from themselves comes forth, they nail it back on the cross where it must be. They are repeatedly applying Christ's death to themselves in order that they might gain Christ and that Christ might grow within them.[21]

These firstfruits give up everything to gain Christ. And, like the apostle Paul, they count it all refuse that they might gain the wonderful person, Christ.[22] Compared to Christ everything is refuse. They see this truth, believe it, and live according to it.

As a consequence, day by day and moment by moment Christ slowly grows within them until He fills and saturates their whole inward being, until there is nothing left within but Christ Himself, until they can say, as the apostle did, "…it is no longer I that live, but Christ liveth in me."[23] Then, in such a condition, they wait for Christ to return, looking for that day when He will come to take them to Himself.

Only a Few

But watch ye at every season, making supplication, that ye may prevail to escape all these things that shall come to pass, and to stand before the Son of man. (Lk. 21:36)

Then shall two men be in the field; one is taken, and one is left: two women shall be grinding at the mill; one is taken, and one is left. (Matt. 24:40-41)

Among the hundreds of millions of believers living on the earth during the endtime, not many will be mature and prepared for the Lord's coming. Not many heed the Lord's word to watch and pray. Many are carried away by the world and the things in the world — by religion, by the flesh, or by one of so many other distractions from Christ.

But there are those who do watch and pray, who will be fully mature and waiting for the Lord at His return. For, two will be in the field; one *will* be taken, while the other is left. Similarly, two will be grinding at the mill; one of those *will* be taken, while the other left. And again, two will be in one bed; one will be taken, the other left.[24] Those taken have spent their lives preparing for that instant when the Lord will come for them.

There will be those who overcome all things through prayer and watchfulness, and in that day are accounted worthy to stand before the Son of Man. These also spend their lives watching and praying at every season. As a consequence they will escape all the trials and turmoil that will afflict the earth during the endtime and stand before the throne of God with their dear Lord.

The church in Philadelphia will also be taken at that time, being kept from the time of trial coming upon the whole earth.[25] They choose a simple life in oneness and love of the brothers. They keep the Lord's word and do not deny His name. They have a little strength. They are not great in power, but the strength of the divine life within them is manifested in their living and in their meeting together. In the Lord's eyes these are most precious. So when He comes, He will steal these away as well. Their love of Him and of each other captures the Lord's heart. He cannot leave them behind.

There are also some in the church in Thyatira who will be taken. This church signifies Roman Catholicism. According to church history that organization fully matches the description of Thyatira. Within her are the deep things of Satan[26] and the woman Jezebel who seduces God's servants to worship idols and commit fornication.[27] But, there are some who overcome this severe degradation. To these the Lord gives the morning star'[28] — the bright light that comes before the dawn of the sun. This is the Christ who comes to His believers secretly, before the dawn, to take them away. This is a reference to rapture before the last three and a half years of this age.

Awaiting Resurrection

...Christ Jesus my Lord: for whom I suffered the loss of all things, and do count them but refuse, that I may gain Christ, and be found in him, not having a righteousness of mine own, even that which is of the law, but that which is through faith in Christ, the righteousness which is from God by faith: that I may know him, and the power of his resurrection, and the fellowship of his sufferings, becoming conformed unto his death; if by any means I may attain unto the resurrection from the dead. (Phil. 3:8-11)

Along with those who are living at the time of the Lord's coming, there are those throughout the centuries who matured but died before the time of the Lord's return. What of these?

The apostle Paul said that he had suffered the loss of all things and counted them to be refuse that he might gain Christ. He desired to know the power of Christ's resurrection and the fellowship of His sufferings, to be conformed to His death, in order that he might by any means *attain* unto the resurrection from the dead.

The resurrection of the dead spoken of in 1 Thessalonians[29] does not require effort on our part to experience. *All* believers who are still in paradise[30] under the earth* at the time the Lord descends to the air will be resurrected. Since Paul desired to *attain* the resurrection of which he spoke, he could not have been referring to the event recorded in 1 Thessalonians. Paul was referring to another resurrection, a special resurrection.

Indeed, the word that he uses for resurrection in Philippians is only used here in the New Testament. It is the word for resurrection prepended with the Greek word "ex," which means "out of." This word is properly translated the "out-resurrection" from the dead. Paul wanted to be raised *out* from the dead. He did not

---

*Contrary to popular opinion, according to the Bible the believers do not go to heaven when they die. On the cross the Lord told the penitent thief that he would be with the Lord in Paradise on that day (Lk. 23:43). But after death the Lord did not ascend to heaven; rather, He went into the lower parts of the earth (Eph. 4:9-10), into Hades (Acts 2:27, 31). As revealed in Luke 16:19-31, there are both pleasant and very unpleasant sections in Hades. It is to the pleasant section that the thief went upon his death and the believers go upon their deaths. There they await resurrection – their *rising from the dead*, not their descending from heaven.

want to simply be one of the dead who are raised. There is a great difference.*

About the same time the living, mature believers are taken by the Lord, those who have died and yet attained to the resurrection out from among the dead will likely be resurrected and taken as well. They, along with the mature living believers, will comprise the firstfruits of God's endtime crop. These are the ones taken before the last three and a half years of this age.

The Harvest

For this we say unto you by the word of the Lord, that we that are alive, that are left unto the coming of the Lord, shall in no wise precede them that are fallen asleep. For the Lord himself shall descend from heaven, with a shout, with the voice of the archangel, and with the trump of God: and the dead in Christ shall rise first; then we that are alive, that are left, shall together with them be caught up in the clouds, to meet the Lord in the air: and so shall we ever be with the Lord. (1 Thes. 4:15-17)

Who, then, are those in the main harvest? In the apostle Paul's word about the rapture of the majority of the Christians in 1 Thessalonians 4, there is a crucial word that is used twice and is largely overlooked or ignored by readers. That word is "left." In describing that event Paul says, "we that are alive, that *are left* unto the coming of the Lord" will not precede those who have fallen asleep. Then he repeats himself, emphasizing his previous word: "then we that are alive, *that are left*," will be caught up in the clouds.

Paul could have simply said "then we who are alive until the coming of the Lord" and "then we who are alive will be caught up in the clouds." That would have been sufficient to include all the living believers in his words. But he wrote carefully. He said we who are alive and are left – left on the earth, left after some have been taken. This is similar to the Lord's word in Matthew: one shall be taken, and the other left.[31] Who, then, comprises the main harvest? It is all those who are left; all those who are not taken when the firstfruits are raptured.

---

*This difference will be explored in some detail in *Chapter 4 – The Means*.

Watch!

And what I say unto you I say unto all, Watch. (Mk. 13:37)

The Lord repeatedly commanded the believers to watch. He warned His disciples and us all to watch. In Matthew, Mark, and Luke He told us to watch.[32] Whether one is taken or one is left at the time of the rapture of the firstfruits depends upon whether one has been watching, and by watching preparing for the Lord's return. To watch is to look away to Him,[33] to behold Him.[34] By doing this we are transformed into the same image. This is growing into maturity, and this prepares us for the Lord's return.

If we do not watch, we cannot mature — it is simply impossible. And foreseeing that some might try to somehow extricate themselves from this requirement by saying this does not apply to the believers, the Lord adds a most emphatic word: "What I say to you I say to all, Watch." The Lord could not be clearer. He is telling all the believers to watch, to look for Him, to look away to Him, to behold Him, to be on guard lest the evil one distract them in some way from Christ Himself, their prize. Unfortunately, many will not heed this word; they will not watch. These will be left behind to pass through the great tribulation.

Not Prevailing

But watch ye at every season, making supplication, that ye may prevail to escape all these things that shall come to pass, and to stand before the Son of man. (Lk. 21:36)

In Luke there are those who are counted worthy, who prevail to stand before the Son of Man and escape all those things coming upon the earth. Then what about those who do not prevail, who are not accounted worthy. They *do not escape* all the things coming upon the earth.

There is no evading the meaning of this verse. Some watch and pray at all times, and in that day will stand before the Son of Man. Others do not watch and do not pray. Rather than stand before the Son of Man, they will pass through the great tribulation to be harvested at the very end of that last three and a half years.

God desires all believers to ripen in a timely fashion, be prepared for the Lord's coming, and be taken to be with Him.

However not all believers do. All the ones who are not firstfruits* constitute the harvest in Revelation 14. As the apostle made clear in 1 Thessalonians, that harvest will include all the remaining believers whether living or dead. The dead believers will be resurrected and then the living, remaining believers will be caught up to the air along with them to meet with the Lord. This is the harvest in Revelation 14.

In Summary

The fully mature New Testament believers, both living and dead at the time of the Lord's return, comprise the firstfruits. These have finished their course,[35] having gained Christ[36] to the fullest. They have been fully transformed into Christ's image, and match Him in every way.

On the other hand, the harvest is composed of all the remaining Christians, all those who are left after the firstfruits have been taken. These will be left to pass through the time of trial that will come upon the whole earth, to wean them from their entanglements with the evil world, bring them back to the simplicity that is in Christ, and help them mature in the divine life.

---

*The manchild is also raptured about the same time as the firstfruits and is a special case. See the Appendix for more detail about the manchild.

References

[1] Jn. 3:6
[2] Col. 3:4; 1 Jn. 5:20
[3] 2 Cor. 3:18
[4] Phil. 3:21; Col. 3:4
[5] Matt. 17:1-2
[6] Rev. 14:1, 3
[7] Gen. 2:10
[8] Ps. 23:2; 46:4; 65:9
[9] Ez. 47:1-5
[10] Jn. 7:38
[11] Gen. 2:9; Rev. 22:2
[12] Jn. 15:1
[13] Jn. 6:32-35
[14] 1 Cor. 5:7
[15] Rev. 22:17
[16] Matt. 7:14
[17] 1 Jn. 2:15
[18] Phil. 3:7-8
[19] Lk. 14:26; Matt. 16:24
[20] Rom. 6:6
[21] Col. 2:19
[22] Phil. 3:8
[23] Gal. 2:20
[24] Matt. 24:40-41
[25] Rev. 3:10
[26] Rev. 2:24
[27] Rev. 2:20
[28] Rev. 2:28
[29] 1 Thes. 4:15-17
[30] Lk. 23:43
[31] Matt. 24:40-41
[32] Matt. 24:42-43; 25:13; Mk. 13:33-37; Lk. 21:36
[33] Heb. 12:2
[34] 2 Cor. 3:18
[35] 2 Tim. 4:7
[36] Phil. 3:8

CHAPTER 2

The Time

The end of this age is marked by a period* of seven years.† That time is split into two sections, each three and a half years. The last section is the time of trial[1] that is about to come upon the whole inhabited earth. It is also frequently called the great tribulation.‡

A short time before that last three and a half years, the sixth seal will be opened and the earth will be shaken. That will be a warning to the inhabitants of the earth of God's impending judgment. It will be a harbinger of the great asteroid strikes that are about to occur during the opening of the seventh seal and the sounding of the first four trumpets.

When the last three and a half years begins, the seventh seal will be opened and the first four trumpets will sound. Giant asteroids and an unprecedented meteor storm will batter the earth. Nearly the entire world will suffer great destruction, much of it total. However, Europe and the area around the Mediterranean will be spared most of that damage.

During that last three and a half years, the fifth trumpet will sound. That "woe," as it is called, will be directed particularly at the Jews. A while later the sixth trumpet will sound – 200 million horsemen from the East will sweep across Asia towards the

---

*These last 7 years are often called *Daniel's seventieth week*, for it is in Daniel 9:27 that this interval is first set forth in the Bible. There it is called a "week," meaning a group of seven or heptad according to the Hebrew, and is the last of seventy such groups. This time period is explained in much greater detail in previous books, particularly in *The Coming End of the Age*.

†These are seven "biblical" years, each consisting of 360 days.

‡The term "great tribulation" is a misnomer when applied to that last three and a half years of this age. The great tribulation is the time of great suffering to the Jews (Matt. 24:15-21), not to the whole world. It is a subset of the time of trial.

Euphrates and the Middle East, killing one-third of mankind as they proceed toward Armageddon.

At the very end of the last seven years, the seventh trumpet will sound and the seven bowls with the last seven plagues of God's wrath will be poured out upon the Antichrist's kingdom. That seventh trumpet — the last trumpet — will sound at the very end of the time of trial, perhaps on the very last day of the seven years. A timeline for these events as well as for the raptures of the firstfruits and the harvest is shown at the end of this chapter.

This seven-year period is the framework upon which all of the endtime happenings hang. It is the basis for understanding the events ending this age.

A Hidden Gathering

And I saw, and behold, the Lamb standing on the mount Zion, and with him a hundred and forty and four thousand, having his name, and the name of his Father, written on their foreheads. And I heard a voice from heaven, as the voice of many waters, and as the voice of a great thunder: and the voice which I heard was as the voice of harpers harping with their harps... These were purchased from among men, to be the firstfruits unto God and unto the Lamb. (Rev. 14:1-2, 4)

And I heard a great voice in heaven, saying, Now is come the salvation, and the power, and the kingdom of our God, and the authority of his Christ: for the accuser of our brethren is cast down, who accuseth them before our God day and night. And they overcame him because of the blood of the Lamb, and because of the word of their testimony; and they loved not their life even unto death. (Rev. 12:10-11)

At the beginning of Revelation 14, 144,000 firstfruits are standing with the Lamb and singing their song to the Father. There are also an unnumbered multitude accompanying them on Mount Zion, for the Word speaks of a voice of many waters, and of great thunder, and of harpers harping along with the singing 144,000. It also says that there are men there who cannot learn that song. When did all these believers come to be there before the Father? It does not say in Revelation 14 — they are just there.

If we look back to Revelation 12, we see the rapture of the manchild.[2] The manchild consists of all the martyrs during the New Testament age. When he is caught up to the throne of God, a war between Michael and his angels and Satan and his forces ensues. This war is initiated by the manchild upon his arrival at the throne of God. However, after Satan is cast from the heavens to the earth, there is a great voice in heaven saying, "The accuser of our brethren is cast down, who accuseth them before our God day and night." Who is speaking these words? And to whom is the speaker talking?

The phrase "our brethren" refers to the manchild, who was caught up to the heavens. It refers to all the martyrs of the New Testament age, for it says that they loved not their lives unto death. They had been slaughtered by the dragon, Satan, who was seeking to "devour" them.[3] Throughout the New Testament age the evil one has been murdering those who bore the testimony of Jesus and testified of the word of God, in an attempt to keep them from maturing and to stop the crop of God's people from ripening. These martyrs are the manchild. But who is speaking? Whose is the great voice that speaks from heaven and to whom does this one speak? And, who is the "our" in the phrase "our brethren?" Clearly, there are some Christians in the heavens already when the manchild arrives.

These must be the 144,000 as well as the multitude with them on Mount Zion. These are all the fully matured believers from the whole New Testament age. These will already be in the heavens by the time the manchild is raptured. Interestingly, the Word does not mention their rapture.

The Moment

And she was delivered of a son, a man child, who is to rule all the nations with a rod of iron: and her child was caught up unto God, and unto his throne. And the woman fled into the wilderness, where she hath a place prepared of God, that there they may nourish her a thousand two hundred and threescore days. (Rev. 12:5-6)

The manchild is caught up to the heavens immediately prior to the last three and a half years of this age, for the Word says that after the rapture of the manchild the woman flees into the wilderness for 1260 days, which is the exact time of the last three and a half years.

The manchild arrives in the heavens immediately prior to the final three and a half years, and when these martyred believers arrive, the firstfruits are there already. When did they arrive?

We have seen in the previous chapter that the firstfruits are composed of all those believers throughout the entire New Testament age, both living and dead, who have fully matured in Christ. In their living Christ has become everything to them. Their entire universe is the wonderful God. They lived a heavenly life on earth. At some point these are taken — taken from the earth to the heavens, from the physical realm to the realm of God, from the temporal to the fully eternal.

When does this occur? At what point in time is the moment of this great change? This is a secret hidden in the Father and a mystery. The Father has kept the time of the gathering of the firstfruits to Himself, hiding it even from the Son.[4] We only know that it occurs some time before the manchild arrives in the heavens, before the last three and a half years of this age.

How long before? No man can say. Indeed, no man knows the day or the hour. Whether it's days, weeks, or even months prior to the last three and a half years, we simply don't know. Even the Son of God doesn't know! That moment is a surprise and gift from the Father to the Son.

At some point in time as the very end of the age nears, the Father will tell the Son, "Now!" Hearing the word for which He had longed for eons, the Lord will respond by gathering the firstfruits into God's house. All the firstfruits will be transferred into the heavenly realm in full. Their hearts, minds, and spirits were there already. For them it will be simply a change for their physical being, the redemption of their bodies.[5]

The believers who had fully matured but then died will be resurrected *out* from among the dead.[6] Along with them the mature living believers will be taken. These, as we have seen, include the one in the field, the one grinding at the mill, and the one in the bed, the overcomers in the church in Philadelphia, the overcomers in the church in Thyatira, the ones counted worthy to stand before the Son of Man, and the Lord only knows how many others. These all will be gathered before the throne of God for God's satisfaction. But much to do with this gathering, including the point in time at which it occurs, is a mystery hidden in God.

Those Who Remain

And I saw, and behold, a white cloud; and on the cloud I saw one sitting like unto a son of man, having on his head a golden crown, and in his hand a sharp sickle. And another angel came out from the temple, crying with a great voice to him that sat on the cloud, Send forth thy sickle, and reap: for the hour to reap is come; for the harvest of the earth is ripe. And he that sat on the cloud cast his sickle upon the earth; and the earth was reaped. (Rev. 14:14-16)

For this we say unto you by the word of the Lord, that we that are alive, that are left unto the coming of the Lord, shall in no wise precede them that are fallen asleep. For the Lord himself shall descend from heaven, with a shout, with the voice of the archangel, and with the trump of God: and the dead in Christ shall rise first; then we that are alive, that are left, shall together with them be caught up in the clouds, to meet the Lord in the air: and so shall we ever be with the Lord. (1 Thes. 4:15-17)

Behold, I tell you a mystery: We all shall not sleep, but we shall all be changed, in a moment, in the twinkling of an eye, at the last trump: for the trumpet shall sound, and the dead shall be raised incorruptible, and we shall be changed. (1 Cor. 15:51-52)

And the sixth poured out his bowl upon the great river, the river Euphrates; and the water thereof was dried up, that the way might be made ready for the kings that come from the sunrising. And I saw coming out of the mouth of the dragon, and out of the mouth of the beast, and out of the mouth of the false prophet, three unclean spirits, as it were frogs: for they are spirits of demons, working signs; which go forth unto the kings of the whole world, to gather them together unto the war of the great day of God, the Almighty. (Behold, I come as a thief. Blessed is he that watcheth, and keepeth his garments, lest he walk naked, and they see his shame.) (Rev. 16:12-15)

And the woman fled into the wilderness, where she hath a place prepared of God, that there they may nourish her a thousand two hundred and threescore days. (Rev. 12:6)

While the time of the rapture of the firstfruits is hidden in God, the time of the reaping of the Christians remaining on earth after the firstfruits are taken is well known and quite apparent. In Revelation 14 the Lord sends forth His sickle to reap this harvest after the persecution of the Antichrist[7] and immediately before the slaughter of the earthly armies at Armageddon.[8] This indicates that the general harvest of Christians will take place near the end of the last three and a half years of this age at the end of the great tribulation.

Furthermore, 1 Thessalonians says that this event occurs at the sounding of a trumpet, of which there are seven in the book of Revelation. In 1 Corinthians the apostle Paul further refines the time of this event. He tells us which of the seven trumpets sounds – the seventh. It is at the sounding of the seventh trumpet, the last trumpet, that the main body of Christians will be caught up to the air to meet with the Lord. This then must occur at the very end of the great tribulation, perhaps even on the very last day of the last three and half years.

Revelation 16 limits the time window for this harvesting even further. The seven bowls of God's wrath are part of the seventh trumpet. All of these seven bowls get poured out upon the Antichrist's kingdom at the very end of the tribulation. However, when the sixth bowl is poured out, the river Euphrates is dried up and the armies of the earth gather to Armageddon for the final battle. The Lord interjects a word of warning and of encouragement here. He tells the believers still on the earth that He is coming as a thief, and blessed is the one who keeps his garments lest others see his shame.

This indicates that the gathering of the majority of Christians to the Lord will occur during the seventh trumpet, at the time that the sixth bowl of God's wrath is poured out on the earth, as the armies of the earth are gathering to Armageddon.

Finally, Revelation 12 tells us that after the manchild is caught up to God's throne, the woman flees to the wilderness where she will be nourished for 1260 days. The woman signifies all of God's redeemed people and the 1260 days are the last three and a half years of this age. During the endtime Christians will flee from persecution into a place the Bible terms "the wilderness." There they will be nourished for the remainder of the endtime. This seems to indicate that their rapture to be with the Lord will not occur until the very last day of the great tribulation, the 1260th day.

As a Thief

Behold, I come as a thief. Blessed is he that watcheth, and keepeth his garments, lest he walk naked, and they see his shame. (Rev. 16:15)

Therefore be ye also ready; for in an hour that ye think not the Son of man cometh. (Matt. 24:44)

Even though the general time frame for this event is clearly documented in the Bible, its exact moment is not. And so the Lord's coming for the believers at that time is still as a thief. It might not be apparent to the many believers on the earth that the end of the age is imminent. The believers that remain will not be in Israel as the armies gather for war. Nor will they be in Europe, for they will have been extirpated from the Antichrist's kingdom. Rather, as depicted in Revelation 12, they will spend the last three and half years in the wilderness being nourished.

Given the condition of the earth due to the great asteroid strikes that occur in the middle of the last seven years, the exact time and date may no longer be obvious to the remaining Christians. It is possible that some information may be transmitted worldwide by shortwave radio or similar means, but that information will be severely limited. The social media and online news feeds we have today will no longer exist. In addition, it may be difficult to glean much information from radio waves that are greatly distorted by the chaos in the Earth's atmosphere that will still be present to a degree from the calamities of the first four trumpets.

As the word of the gathering of the armies of the earth to Armageddon does spread, the wise among the believers will know the Lord's coming for them is imminent. Then the Lord's word in Revelation 16 will become a great encouragement and reassurance to those who have used the last three and half years to seek Him, and a warning to those who have not. It will be a source of supply to the believers who have been greatly suffering during the endtime. They will be watching for the Lord; their hearts and minds will be prepared to meet with the dear Lord with great hope and anticipation. This will be the opposite of the gathering of the firstfruits, for whom the Lord will come in a totally unexpected moment.

In Summary

The rapture of the firstfruits occurs some time before the last three and a half years of this age. We know nothing more than that. It could be days, months, or even years before. We simply don't know. The rapture of the firstfruits will come in an hour when the believers "think not." It will be completely unanticipated. No one either among the believers or mankind in general will be expecting that event.

The rapture of the majority of Christians, however, occurs at a well-defined time. This transpires during the sounding of the seventh trumpet at the very end of the great tribulation after the pouring out of the sixth bowl of God's wrath, as the armies of the earth are gathering to Armageddon. It will probably occur within a day or two of the very end of the age, and very possibly happen on the last day of the endtime. While the exact moment of that event is unknown, the time window for its occurrence is very narrow.

The diagram below gives a timeline showing the raptures of the firstfruits and harvest with God's judgments during the final years of this age.

The Time 27

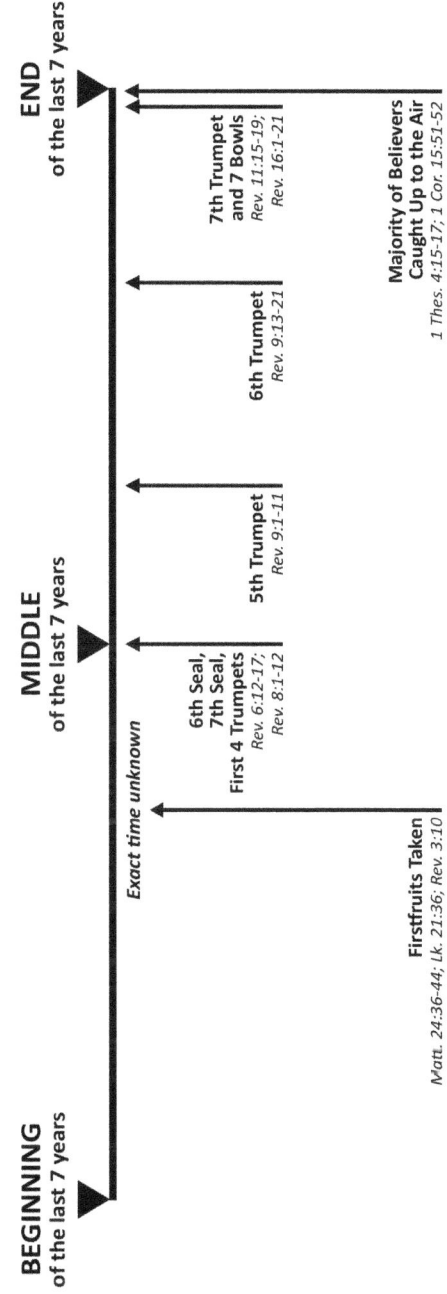

References

[1] Rev. 3:10
[2] Rev. 12:5
[3] Rev. 12:4
[4] Matt. 24:36
[5] Rom. 8:23
[6] Phil. 3:11
[7] Rev. 14:9-13
[8] Rev. 14:17-20

CHAPTER 3

The Place

To where are the believers taken when they are raptured? As we shall see, the place of rapture is different for the firstfruits and the harvest. This corresponds to the different condition of the firstfruits and the harvest. It is a serious error to blindly believe that at the end of this age the Lord will rapture all the believers at the same time to the heavens to stand before God. Such a grievous mistake often leads Christians into a dangerous condition of complacency.

For, if it is true that all are taken together at the same time, to the same place, and are somehow magically changed at the time of the rapture into the kind of person who can stand before God, then what does it matter how a Christian lives on the earth during this age? Whether one loves the world or not, it would not matter. Whether one sins or not would not matter. Whether one follows the Lord are not, how would it matter? We all would be changed at the time of the rapture and everything would be fine. The depth and breadth of this deception are extraordinary; it must be exposed for what it is — an error from the evil one intended to keep Christians from God and from the maturity that would both satisfy God's heart and spell the end of the satanic rule.

So then, consider the place to which the believers are taken. Understand that the place of rapture correlates with the condition of the believers, and is reflective of that.

The Throne of God

And I saw, and behold, the Lamb standing on the mount Zion, and with him a hundred and forty and four thousand, having his name, and the name of his Father, written on their foreheads. And I heard a voice from heaven, as the voice of many waters, and as the voice of a great thunder: and the voice which I heard was as the voice of harpers harping with their harps: and they sing as it were a new song before the throne... (Rev. 14:1-3)

And she was delivered of a son, a man child, who is to rule all the nations with a rod of iron: and her child was caught up unto God, and unto his throne.... And I heard a great voice in heaven, saying, Now is come the salvation, and the power, and the kingdom of our God, and the authority of his Christ: for the accuser of our brethren is cast down, who accuseth them before our God day and night. (Rev. 12:5, 10-11)

In Revelation 14 the firstfruits are seen standing with the Lamb on the heavenly Mount Zion before the throne of God, and in Revelation 12 they are before the throne celebrating the coming of the kingdom of God to the heavens when the manchild is raptured and Satan is cast out. What is the throne of God, and what does it mean to stand before it?

God is Spirit;[1] He is not physical. Consequently, we must not think that His throne is a physical thing. It is not. The throne of God is a spiritual reality. It depicts God who due to His kingly nature rules not just the universe, but everything. His righteous nature is manifested through His authority to be the throne on which He sits. His throne is not a physical thing. His throne is the spiritual reality of His Being in His righteousness and kingship. It is His eternal state of being that is seen as a throne in the spiritual realm (and is in fact the reality of physical thrones).

The Eternal State

After these things I saw, and behold, a great multitude, which no man could number, out of every nation and of all tribes and peoples and tongues, standing before the throne and before the Lamb, arrayed in white robes, and palms in their hands; and they cry with a great voice, saying, Salvation unto our God who sitteth on the throne, and unto the Lamb. (Rev. 7:9-10)

...even as he chose us in him before the foundation of the world, that we should be holy and without blemish before him in love... (Eph. 1:4)

What does it mean to stand before the throne of God? Consider Revelation 6-7. There the sixth seal is opened, the earth is shaken by an enormous earthquake, and the stars fall from the sky. Before the opening of the seventh seal, however, there is an insertion — 144,000 Jews are sealed by God. This event marks a great change, from the age of the Church back to Israel.

This event indicates that the fullness of the Gentiles has come in,[2] and that God has turned back to Israel to bear His testimony[3] on the earth. The sealed Jews are those who will testify of Christ to Israel during the last three and a half years of this age. The time for the nations to believe in Christ, receive Him, and be born again of Him will have ended. The age of grace will be over. God will turn back to Israel not only for His testimony, but also to deal with the unbelief and godlessness in Israel as a whole.

Seeing this, one might ask a pertinent question: now that God has turned back to Israel, what was the whole church age for? What did it produce? The answer to that question is in Revelation 7. There we see a multitude, which no man can number, standing before the throne of God. Only God can count how many they are.

Who are these? Some have made the mistake of thinking that these verses depict the rapture of the New Testament believers to the heavens before the great tribulation. Such an understanding, however, is refuted by the ensuing chapters of Revelation.[4] While these verses may indicate that the rapture has started by that time, they absolutely do not indicate that all the believers have been taken to the heavens. Not only is such an understanding refuted by Revelation itself, it is also contradicted by the writings of the apostle Paul.[5]

Who, then, are these? These are the result of the church age. These are all the Christians throughout all the centuries, whom God has redeemed and brought through His process of salvation, that they might stand before His throne, robed in white and fully approved by Him. These are the sons of God. What did the church age produce? It produced the innumerable sons of God!

This great multitude corresponds to those in Ephesians 1 who are before God in Christ. To stand before the God who sits on His throne is a momentous matter. Who could possibly stand before the throne of the righteous God, passing God's judgment?

Aside from Christ, who is worthy to stand in such a position? And yet this innumerable multitude is there!

What do these verses describe? They show us the eternal state of all the Christians from throughout the entire church age. What is the result of the church age? It is this innumerable multitude standing before the throne of God in eternity as His many glorified sons, who are like His only begotten Son in every way. What did the church age produce? The many glorified sons of God.

In eternity the many sons of God are before His throne in love. They have been brought from the lowest state, from the earth, the fall, and from corrupted humanity, to the highest state possible – in Christ, before God's throne of righteousness, enjoying God's love. This is the eternal state of every Christian.

However, the firstfruits reach this state, this condition first. They are enjoying the eternal state in Revelation 14, before the last three and a half years of this age. They have attained that eternal goal by ripening before the main harvest. What does it mean to stand before the throne of God? It means to attain the eternal state to which every Christian is predestined.

The Righteous Judge

I have fought the good fight, I have finished the course, I have kept the faith: henceforth there is laid up for me the crown of righteousness, which the Lord, the righteous judge, shall give to me at that day; and not to me only, but also to all them that have loved his appearing. (1 Tim. 4:7-8)

To stand before the throne of God also means to match God in His righteousness. It means to be the same as God in righteousness in every respect. When the firstfruits stand before His throne the righteous God will see nothing to judge.

To stand before God's throne is to meet the divine standard of righteousness. It is to be perfect and complete in every way, like the Father is.[6] This is *not* simply to do no wrong, to be *sinlessly* perfect. It is far more. Like Christ, this is to express God, to shine out God, to flow God out in every circumstance and under all conditions. It is this expression of God seen first in the Only Begotten, then in the firstfruits, and eventually in God's many sons in eternity that God sees as right, as meeting His righteousness. Nothing short of this divine expression qualifies one to stand before God's throne.

This is not due to the self-effort of the firstfruits. Rather, it is due to their constant seeking and gaining of Christ, so that He grows in them and is lived out through them. They manifest Him and that manifestation is their righteousness. God sees no fault and no unrighteousness in them – He sees Christ expressed through them. The very Son of God in whom God is well pleased[7] is lived out through these firstfruits, and this living of Christ is, in fact, God's perfect righteousness.

Transcendent

To be before the throne of God is to transcend every human problem, the entire human condition, every type of situation, the fall, the natural man, and everything that is not God Himself. There is nothing higher than the throne of God. To be there is to be in the highest possible position. It is to be brought from the lowest of earthly states to the highest, divine state. To be before the throne of God is to have transcended everything and been brought fully into God Himself.

A Change of Realm

Finally, the firstfruits will be transferred to the heavenly and spiritual Mount Zion. They will be mysteriously transported into the spiritual and mystical realm of God Himself, even as the Lord was in His resurrection and ascension. Their spirit and heart are there already; when they are taken, their bodies will also be changed into spiritual bodies, to match the Lord Jesus in every way. However, we simply do not yet know what that will be.[8]

To the Air

For the Lord himself shall descend from heaven, with a shout, with the voice of the archangel, and with the trump of God: and the dead in Christ shall rise first; then we that are alive, that are left, shall together with them be caught up in the clouds, to meet the

Lord in the air: and so shall we ever be with the Lord. (1 Thes. 4:16-17)

And I saw, and behold, a white cloud; and on the cloud I saw one sitting like unto a son of man, having on his head a golden crown, and in his hand a sharp sickle. (Rev. 14:14)

Let both grow together until the harvest: and in the time of the harvest I will say to the reapers, Gather up first the tares, and bind them in bundles to burn them; but gather the wheat into my barn. (Matt. 13:30)

While the firstfruits are taken to the throne of God, the majority of believers are raptured elsewhere. In his epistle to the Thessalonians Paul is quite specific about this. He says that the Lord will first descend from the heavens with the voice of the archangel and the trumpet of God. Having descended, He will resurrect the dead believers. Then those who are alive along with the resurrected believers will be caught up to meet with the Lord *in the air*. Paul is clear and precise. When the majority of the believers are caught up to meet with the Lord, He has left the heavens and descended to the air.

Revelation 14 tells us essentially the same thing. There the Son of Man, the Lord Jesus, is on a *cloud* when He reaps the harvest of the believers from the earth. Being on a cloud indicates that He has descended to the air from the throne of God in the heavens. It also indicates that the harvest will be brought to Him where He is, in the air. This confirms the apostle's word about the place of the rapture of the majority of believers.

Furthermore, the Lord Himself speaks something similar. In Matthew 13 He says at the time of harvest He will send forth His reapers to gather His wheat into His barn. This harvest will not be brought into His house; it is the firstfruits that are brought into the house of God.[9] The harvest will be brought into the barn, the place where grain is stored for later use.

The majority of the New Testament believers are not taken to the throne of God; they are caught up to the air to stand before the Lord. There they will answer to the Lord at His judgment seat for what they have done while in their bodies, whether good or bad.[10]

A Change of Physical Position

While the firstfruits will be transferred into the mystical realm when they are taken, the harvest will be caught up in the clouds to the air, to a physical place. Not only is the destination of the harvest's rapture different from that of the firstfruits, the *realm* is different. The firstfruits will be transported mysteriously into the spiritual realm, while the harvest will merely change physical position. They are not yet ready for the spiritual realm.

The Lord's Wisdom

The Lord could conceivably take the remaining believers at the end of the tribulation from the earth to the heavens to meet with Him there, before descending to the air. However, He will wait until He descends. Why would He do this? It is because all these believers will not yet be ready to stand before God as He sits upon His throne. There still will be more to accomplish in them — in some believers there will be quite much, while in others less. But these believers will not be fully mature. As such they will not be able to stand before the righteous God based upon their own inward condition in Christ.

The Lord knows the condition of each and every believer. He knows our needs, our shortages, and the discrepancies between us and God. During this age He clothes us with Himself as our righteousness objectively,[11] that we might come forward to God to the throne of grace for timely help,[12] that we might partake of what God is, in order that He become our inward strength, supply, and our very person. It is by drawing near to God that we are changed day by day into Christ's likeness. As this process progresses, the Christ within us grows and is slowly manifested in our daily lives, in our deeds, in our works. This Christ who is lived out from within us becomes our righteousness *subjectively*. It is this subjective Christ manifested from within us that will enable us to stand before the throne of God.

The age of grace will end at the Lord's coming. The age of the kingdom will take its place. At that time our access to God will be of a different character. The time of freely coming forward to God to partake of Him that He might meet our every need will change. Many will be in outer darkness where there will be weeping and gnashing of teeth.[13] This is not a description of our current experience of God, but does describe the experience of those Christians who are greatly lacking in the next age.

Consequently, the Lord in His wisdom, knowing the condition of all the believers left on earth, brings them to the air, not to the throne of God. He still will have work to do within these believers, and in some cases much work to do.

In this age if we cooperate with the Lord fully and give Him the freedom to move within us however He sees fit, He will bring us to full maturity in His life and to the throne of God. But if we don't cooperate, He can't do this. Therefore, in the coming age there will be the need for Him to do something more.

At that time it will not be a matter of us cooperating, for we will no longer be given a choice. He will deal with us as is needed for our good to bring us into the eternal state. And so the Lord will bring all the remaining believers to the air as a kind of interim keeping place. Then, during the millennium, He will finish the process He began in the believers, bringing them into their eternal position before the throne of God.

The Sea of Glass

...before the throne, as it were a sea of glass like unto crystal... (Rev. 4:6)

And I saw as it were a sea of glass mingled with fire; and them that come off victorious from the beast, and from his image, and from the number of his name, standing by the sea of glass, having harps of God. (Rev. 15:2)

In the days of Noah, God judged the whole earth with water. Only Noah, his family, and the animals Noah brought with him into the ark passed through that water-judgment. Similarly, before God's throne there is a sea of glass. It is with this sea that everything is judged.

To stand before the throne of God one must be able to pass through the judgment of the sea of glass. Buried within that sea is everything that is not according to God, including the world, the flesh, sin, and even our own selves. That sea of glass is the repository for all things negative, for all things not according to God's nature.

Noah passed through the flood by building an ark according to God's specifications. That ark is a type of Christ, but it is the Christ whom we *build*. It is the Christ we experience in our daily life who is deposited within us over time and who, being built up within us, eventually becomes our subjective salvation from judgment.

By the end of Revelation that sea of glass is mingled with fire.* God's judgment will change. It will no longer be a matter of simply burying what is negative, but rather of consuming it with fire. As seen in Revelation 15, to stand before the throne of God one must be able to stand upon that sea of glass mingled with fire. That means to have nothing left in our being that requires judgment.

It should now be apparent why the Lord brings the majority of believers to the air. There will still be something in these believers not yet according to God, something that requires further work by the Lord to eliminate. Furthermore, additional growth of the divine life and spreading of the divine nature within these believers will be required, to expunge all that will eventually be judged under the sea of glass.

In Summary

The firstfruits are taken to the throne of God. They match Christ in every respect and stand before the One on the throne, where the righteousness of the Christ is manifested from within them in full and they are a sweet satisfaction to the Father. They will shine like the sun in their Father's kingdom.[14]

The harvest of the majority of believers at the very end of this age is of a different character. In this harvest the believers are caught up to the air to meet with the Lord; they are not brought to the throne of God. The Lord will descend from the heavens and meet in the air with all the remaining Christians. There the Lord

---

* The sea of glass mingled with fire will eventually become the lake of fire in eternity. There all things negative will be consumed eternally.

will pass judgment on each believer regarding their status during the coming kingdom age.[15]

References

[1] Jn. 4:24
[2] Rom. 11:25
[3] Rev. 7:2-8; 12:17
[4] For example, Rev. 14:14-16; 16:15
[5] 1 Thes. 4:16-17; 1 Cor. 15:52
[6] Matt. 5:48
[7] Matt. 3:17; 17:5
[8] 1 Jn. 3:2
[9] Ex. 23:19
[10] 2 Cor. 5:10
[11] 1 Cor. 1:30
[12] Heb. 4:16
[13] Matt. 22:13; 25:30
[14] Matt. 13:43
[15] Rom. 14:10; 2 Cor. 5:10; Matt. 25:14-30; Lk. 12:41-48

CHAPTER 4

The Means

The firstfruits and the harvest are the same in life and nature. All Christians share the Father's divine life, which is Christ Himself.[1] All Christians partake of the same divine nature.[2] Every Christian is gifted in some manner or another from the Lord.[3] We all have been given one or more talents to invest for the Lord.[4] We all have access to the same God in the same one Spirit.[5] Furthermore, God shows no partiality in His dealings with each of us.[6]

However, there is one major difference between the firstfruits and the harvest. The firstfruits avail themselves of all that God is and provides in order to gain Christ, grow in Him, and attain the high calling of God in Christ. To one degree or another the harvest does not. Because of this the firstfruits ripen in a timely manner, before the time of trial comes upon the earth. The harvest, on the other hand, does not. Consequently, the believers comprising the harvest will pass through great suffering during the endtime to help them grow in Christ.

This difference in maturity in the divine life is revealed in the various aspects of the rapture. As we have seen, the firstfruits and the harvest are not raptured at the same time: the former will be taken before the tribulation, whereas the latter will be taken at the end. They are also not raptured to the same place. The firstfruits will be taken to the throne of God in the heavenly and spiritual realm to appear before the Father. They are brought into the house of God for God's satisfaction. The harvest, however, is caught up to the physical air.

It should be no surprise then that there is a great difference in the means through which the firstfruits and harvest are gathered from the earth. When I speak of the "means" by which the believers are gathered, I am talking about the mechanism the Lord uses to reap the believers from the earth. This mechanism is not the same for the firstfruits and harvest.

Taken

...so shall be the coming of the Son of man. Then shall two men be in the field; one is taken, and one is left: two women shall be grinding at the mill; one is taken, and one is left. (Matt. 24:39-41)

I say unto you, In that night there shall be two men on one bed; the one shall be taken, and the other shall be left. There shall be two women grinding together; the one shall be taken, and the other shall be left. (Lk. 17:34-35)

The Greek word (paralambano) translated "taken" in these verses means to receive or to take to or with oneself. For example, it is used when referring to the taking of a wife.[7] Given the mystery surrounding this the rapture of the firstfruits, it's as if the Lord is secretly coming to take away a bride. There is an implication of intimacy in the Lord's choice of words. And, He does not carry her away. Rather, He comes and they leave together.

When the Lord comes for the firstfruits it will not be a spectacular event — it will not be ostentatious in any way. It will be hardly noticeable. That coming will be secret, hidden, mysterious. There may be some very brief manifestation of glory as the firstfruits are transfigured and taken from the earth and the physical realm. But if there is, it will be so brief as to be barely perceptible. The Lord will be coming for His lovers, not to convince the world of His divinity.

At this secret coming, the Lord will speak to the heart of the believers. He will call each by name. Those who are ready, who have been watching for His return, will immediately and unreservedly respond to His call. There will be no need for them to let go of anything, for they will have already left behind everything for Christ. When called by the Lord, they will come. They will come out of the whole physical sphere into that spiritual realm from which their dear Lord calls. Their bodies will change to be like His body. They will join the One whom they love, and together they will ascend to the throne of God.

Leaning upon the Beloved

Who is this that cometh up from the wilderness, Leaning upon her beloved? (SS. 8:5)

This sweet departure of Christ and His lovers from the earth at the time of His secret coming is reminiscent of a passage from Song of Songs. There one asks, "Who is this that comes up out of the wilderness leaning upon her beloved?" Early in the Song of Songs the seeking one was a steed in Pharaoh's chariot;[8] she was pulling behind her the world with its ruler. Sometime later she held her beloved and would not let him go.[9] By the end of the Song of Songs she is simply leaning on her beloved. She is fully trusting in him for everything. If he moves away, she will fall; but she knows he will never move away. They are joined.

And so it is when the firstfruits are taken. They will lean upon the Lord, fully trusting in Him. Together they will come to the throne of God, to present themselves before the Father. Her long time on the earth in the flesh will have come to an end. She will leave her "wilderness" to be with the dear Lord Jesus fully and eternally.

The Power of His Person

...the power of an endless life... (Heb. 7:16)

...whom God raised up, having loosed the pangs of death: because it was not possible that he should be holden of it. (Acts 2:24)

When the Lord resurrected and ascended, He did not do so by the power of God coming upon Him externally, objectively. Rather, it was through the power of the indestructible life – the life of God – within Him that He rose from the dead. It was simply not possible for death to hold Him. And when He ascended it was not that the Spirit caught Him up, taking Him from the earth. This would have been something objective, something working upon Him. The Lord Jesus had no need of such an external force, for it was by the power of His own Person that He ascended through all the heavens.[10]

When He secretly comes to take the firstfruits, He will energize His life within them. This life will break forth[11] from within their human shell, transfiguring their bodies from within,[12] changing them from natural to spiritual bodies in the process. They will then be like the Lord in every way, even in body.

They will then ascend. However, this ascension will not be like what the apostle Paul experienced when he was caught up to the third heaven.[13] It will not be due to an external force. Rather, this ascension will transpire by the power of the Person of Christ within the firstfruits, just as when the Lord ascended after His resurrection. They will ascend with the Lord who calls them, to the throne of God by the power of His Person within them.

The Out-Resurrection

...if by any means I may attain unto the resurrection from the dead. (Phil. 3:11)

I believe at the same time as the living mature believers are taken, those Christians who have matured and died throughout the centuries will be resurrected and also taken. As mentioned previously, Paul spoke of attaining a special resurrection, an "ex-resurrection." He foresaw the prize[14] of this secret resurrection and ascension to the throne of God.

This ex-resurrection is a special resurrection, an "extra" resurrection. The resurrection in 1 Thessalonians[15] is one accomplished by the power of God upon the believers who have died. It is an objective raising of the dead believers, like the resurrection of Lazarus, when the Lord called him forth from the grave by the word of His power. The resurrection which Paul sought to attain is something different. It is a resurrection like Christ's. It is accomplished by the working of the divine life within us. It is a subjective raising of the believers, *out* from death through the power of the indestructible life of Christ within us.

This is how Christ rose. He rose from the dead because it was not possible for Him to be bound by it. He was constituted according to the power of an indestructible life. Death could not hold Him. In the same way at the endtime, when the Lord energizes and exercises His life within the mature believers, they cannot be held by death. There are no bonds that can keep them in the grave.

The Reality

When Christ, who is our life, shall be manifested, then shall ye also with him be manifested in glory. (Col. 3:4)

God has put us into Christ.[16] When Christ rose from the dead, we rose with Him.[17] When Christ ascended, we ascended in Him.[18] In Christ we have been made to sit in the heavenly places.[19] This is the spiritual reality and these are spiritual facts. They can never be undone. They have been accomplished once for all by Christ in His death, resurrection, and ascension.

However, our experience of these facts varies. Before we first come to the Lord, we have no experience of this spiritual reality. In eternity future every Christian will be before the throne of God. We will experience these spiritual facts to the full. That reality will be our experience. Between the time of our initial salvation and eternity future there is a long process. God is slowly transferring our awareness, our consciousness, our very being from the earth to the heavenly places, from the merely physical to the spiritual and mystical realm of God, from the creation to God himself.

As we pass through this process we begin to see and realize just how many things bind us to the earth, tie us to the world, and keep us from experiencing the spiritual reality. As the Lord said, "Where your treasure is, there will your heart be also."[20] As we slowly mature in Christ we see just how many things our heart is attached to. How many things other than God do we love, do we treasure, do we desire? If we are honest with ourselves our answer would be, "Far too many." Even one is too many!

How can we stand before God at His throne when our heart is elsewhere? If I love the world, how can I stand before the throne of God. If my heart is elsewhere, I am elsewhere. The throne of God is not a physical place or physical position. It is a state of being, a spiritual reality. If I am loving the world I am not in the spiritual reality of the throne of God. It's quite simple. We cannot have both. We cannot serve two masters.[21] Our love of something other than God negates the experience of God.

As we grow in Christ and our love for Him increases, the things to which our heart is attached begin to fall away. One by one the bonds that hold us on the earth and this physical sphere are dissolved. What once was so important to us becomes essentially meaningless to our existence. Our relationships with the things on the earth, the things in the world, and the people in our lives change. We become no longer bound by all the earthly ties.

Even our physical relationships change. Our parents, siblings, and relatives change in our experience. Recall what the Lord said: "He that loveth father or mother more than me is not worthy of me; and he that loveth son or daughter more than me is not worthy of me."[22] And, "If any man cometh unto me, and hateth not his own father, and mother, and wife, and children, and brethren, and sisters, yea, and his own life also, he cannot be my disciple."[23] All these earthly relationships do not exist in the God's spiritual realm. They are and were temporary, used by God to bring us into existence, but then to be left behind as we travel toward our ultimate goal of the eternal state.

As we grow in Christ, those things that are not the reality fall away one by one. As we mature in Christ the worldly things lose their hold upon us. We no longer love them nor are we attached to them. The earthly and the natural things also lose their power to constrain us. We were raised in them and part of them, but no longer. We are being called out of all these into God Himself and into our eternal position in and before Him.

As we near full maturity in Christ our love for Him intensifies. We love God with all our heart. Nothing can supplant that love within us. He is our desire; He is our goal; He is our real love. Everything else slowly disappears. But, we find there is one thing tying us to this physical, earthly realm from which we seemingly cannot escape – our physical bodies.

Our physical bodies hold us to the earth. They demand our time and attention. As we get older, death slowly works in our bodies. We watch it slowly corrupting our physical being. One malady after another attacks us. One problem after another afflicts our bodies. However, even many of these physical ties are slowly overcome; even these cannot keep us from God. But, the physical body with our attachment to it remains.

When the Lord comes for the firstfruits, He will come for them from within. The Christ who is their *life* will be manifested. This will change their physical body to be like the Lord's. The last attachment holding the firstfruits to this physical realm will disappear. They will spontaneously, automatically, without any effort whatsoever enter into the full experience of the spiritual reality of the eternal state.

Before their transfiguration, the heart of the firstfruits will be fully in this state already, but their bodies will still be on the earth. When their bodies are changed their whole being will enter into the eternal spiritual reality in Christ. They will be transferred to the heavens; they will enter into the spiritual reality in full; they will be changed to be identical with Christ in every way. These are all different aspects of the same thing – standing before the throne of God.

The rapture of the firstfruits is simply the spontaneous change that results from Christ as life spreading from their spirit into the soul, and then at maturity from the soul into their body. For the firstfruits their heart was already before the throne of God, loving the Father. The change of their bodies is simply the last step in the process of bringing forth sons of God from what was once merely creation.

The firstfruits can be likened to caterpillars. Caterpillars are earthbound, crawling upon the dirt, shrubs, and trees. But at some point they form a chrysalis. In that state they undergo a metabolic change and are slowly transformed. Then one day the chrysalis cracks; the shell breaks. They emerge from the chrysalis and spontaneously fly!

This is the natural process of the butterfly. It is similar to the "natural" process of a son of God. If a believer is properly nourished in Christ and continues on the proper path of the spiritual life, there will come the day when that which is within him will burst forth, breaking the "shell" in a sense. Then, without any effort the believer simply "flies." Our natural state of being will be in the heavens at the throne of God enjoying all that He has prepared for us.

Left

...For our passover also hath been sacrificed, even Christ: wherefore let us keep the feast... (1 Cor. 5:7-8)

The majority of the believers living on the earth during the final years of this age will be left behind to pass through the great tribulation.* They will be in the "wilderness," in a place prepared by God for them.²⁴ There they will be nourished for 1260 days. That they will be *nourished* during that time indicates that they are undernourished now. The problem with so many believers today is the lack of proper nourishment, proper spiritual food.

Today in so many places the believers are not being fed proper food. In many cases they are being fed spiritual baby food day after day, week after week. They are not being provided with solid food, the spiritual meat which will enable them to grow.²⁵ They are not being fed with all the spiritual nutrients found in the Christ who is our rich feast. As a consequence their growth has been stunted. They have become spiritually underdeveloped and malnourished.

In other places they are being fed a kind of synthetic food, a spiritual diet that has no nutritional value whatsoever. It may appear to be something of value, but in fact it is void of Christ. It has a certain appearance, yet is altogether without substance. It is a man-made substance which totally lacks God. As the believers eat this kind of food, they slowly become increasingly malnourished and underdeveloped. Their spiritual being with its spiritual muscles atrophies; all the spiritual strength and vigor that came with their rebirth is sapped away. Thousands upon thousands, perhaps millions upon millions, suffer in the pews, wasting away under the Christ-less teachings being spoon-fed to them. When the endtime comes how could these possibly be ready? They have not been eating solid spiritual food or drinking the real spiritual drink. They are famished, and for the most part don't even realize it.

This lack of nourishment results in serious problems. How many Christian brothers and sisters love the world? Why do they love the world? Because they are starving; they are not eating the

---

*Properly speaking, as mentioned before, the great tribulation refers to the time of immense suffering Israel will pass through during the last three and a half years of this age. This period is also called the time of Jacob's trouble (Jer. 30:7). The intensity of that suffering is needed for Israel to turn from its godlessness, unbelief, and hatred of Christ back to God and their Messiah. That unprecedented suffering will not be the lot of the believers left on the earth. However, these years will be a time of great suffering and trial for them. Indeed, the Bible calls it the time of trial (Rev. 3:10). Yet, it will not compare to what Israel will pass through.

proper spiritual food. They are without the spiritual strength and content of Christ to overcome the world. Without the proper food how can their spiritual life and their love of God grow?

So many believers are trapped by the flesh or earthly things. Why? Because their spiritual life is greatly undernourished. They need to be fed — fed with Christ Himself. Daily they need to experience the Christ who is food to them.[26] They need the wonderful, life-giving Spirit of God as a flowing river to quench their thirst.[27] This is not a doctrine. This is an experience and a spiritual reality. Doctrines cannot nourish our spiritual being. Only Christ Himself as the Spirit[28] can nourish us and slake the thirst of God's children.

Unfortunately, by the endtime the majority of Christians will still be spiritual infants.[29] They will not have matured. They will not be full-grown in Christ.[30] When the Lord comes secretly, they will not be able to respond properly because they will still be babes, bound to the earth and to this world by innumerable ties. And so, they will be left behind to pass through the time of trial.

The Harvesters

And I saw, and behold, a white cloud; and on the cloud I saw one sitting like unto a son of man, having on his head a golden crown, and in his hand a sharp sickle. And another angel came out from the temple, crying with a great voice to him that sat on the cloud, Send forth thy sickle, and reap: for the hour to reap is come; for the harvest of the earth is ripe. And he that sat on the cloud cast his sickle upon the earth; and the earth was reaped. (Rev. 14:14-16)

Let both grow together until the harvest: and in the time of the harvest I will say to the reapers, Gather up first the tares, and bind them in bundles to burn them; but gather the wheat into my barn. ... and the reapers are angels. (Matt. 13:30, 38)

At the very end of the age the time of harvest will come. The Lord will thrust in His sickle and reap the earth of all the remaining believers. This will include those who have died and those who are alive. These all will be caught up to the air to meet with the Christ.

How does the Lord accomplish this? This will not be like the experience of the firstfruits. The firstfruits will pass fully into the spiritual realm to the throne of God, when their last bond to the earth — their physical body — is changed. This is accomplished by the power of the divine life within them. They will ascend with Christ to the throne of God by the power of Christ's Person within them.

This is not the case with the majority of believers. The Lord specifically tells us that He will send forth His angels to reap the endtime harvest. The sickle that the Lord uses to reap the earth is His angels.

The firstfruits have no need of angelic help to ascend to the throne of God. However, the believers in the harvest require the angels to transport them to the air to meet with Christ. Why? Because they still have not been fully freed from all the earthly bonds.

Consider: all these dear brothers and sisters will not have overcome the world in their experience. How many of them will still love the world* when the endtime comes? They did not overcome the world, nor did they overcome themselves. They were still attached to so many things on the earth and in the physical realm. It will require the last three and a half years of suffering to start to deal with these many attachments.

It will not be that they experienced Christ and through this experience overcame these things. Rather, it will be that all of these will be *taken away* from them during that last three and a half years. They will be in a wilderness! All these worldly and earthly enjoyments and distractions from God will be destroyed, gone, unavailable. They will not have overcome them; God will have destroyed them all for their benefit.

So then, when the time of harvest comes, they still will not have attained that eternal state of being depicted by the throne of God. In order to bring them to meet with the Lord in the air, the help of the angels will be needed. An external force will have to be applied to them to rapture them in the clouds to meet with the Lord.

---

*Understand that *every* aspect of Satan's working upon the earth is part of the world, including *religion*.

This difference between the firstfruits and the harvest is striking. The firstfruits ascend unaided to the heavens. That is simply one of the functions of the divine life and divine nature being manifested in the mature sons of God.

The harvest has not yet reached that level of maturity. While many believers will grow in Christ significantly during the endtime, many will not. But, in either case, it will require the exercise of external helpers, the angels, to reap the believers from the earth to meet with the Lord in the air.

Caught Up, Caught Away

And when they came up out of the water, the Spirit of the Lord caught away Philip; and the eunuch saw him no more, for he went on his way rejoicing. (Acts 8:39)

I know a man in Christ, fourteen years ago (whether in the body, I know not; or whether out of the body, I know not; God knoweth), such a one caught up even to the third heaven. And I know such a man (whether in the body, or apart from the body, I know not; God knoweth), how that he was caught up into Paradise…(2 Cor. 2-4)

And she was delivered of a son, a man child, who is to rule all the nations with a rod of iron: and her child was caught up unto God, and unto his throne. (Rev. 12:5)

…then we that are alive, that are left, shall together with them be caught up in the clouds, to meet the Lord in the air: and so shall we ever be with the Lord. (1 Thes. 4:17)

It is said of the believers that they will be caught up to the air to meet with the Lord. This verb, "caught up," is distinctly different from the word used for the firstfruits. The firstfruits are *taken*. They are reccived by the Lord and then go with the Lord. It is a kind of mutual and intimate going together.

However, the harvest is *caught up*. This verb is used in other places in the New Testament. When Philip was transported after preaching the gospel to the eunuch, the Spirit of God caught Philip away. In Philip's case the Spirit as an external force upon him transported him from one location to another. This was not done by the life of God within Philip, but by the power of God upon him.

In 2 Corinthians Paul uses this word twice. In one instance he speaks about being caught up to the third heaven. In another instance he speaks of being caught away* to Paradise.† In both these instances the apostle was transported by an external force upon him, once to the third heaven and the other time to Paradise.

This verb, as applied to the believers in 1 Thessalonians, indicates that they are being transported from the earth to the air by an external force. According to Matthew 13, that external force is the angels. How different the rapture of the firstfruits and the harvest is!

In Summary

The firstfruits are the mature believers at the time of the Lord's secret coming at the end of this age. Those mature believers who have died will enjoy the death-overcoming, resurrecting life of Christ within them lifting them from the grave. Then all the mature believers will join the Lord to ascend to the heavens and God's throne. This will be accomplished by the transcendent power of the Christ within them as He overcomes the final bond that ties these believers to the earth — that is, as He transfigures their bodies.

The rapture of the harvest is quite different. The harvest will not yet be ready to experience the throne of God and so will be brought to the air. This is accomplished not by the divine life within them, but rather by the angels, who will be sent by Christ to harvest the believers. In the case of the firstfruits, it is God working within them as life subjectively that brings them to the throne of God. In the case of the harvest, it is the external power of the angels upon them that transports them to the air to be with Christ.

---

*This word can be translated either caught up or caught away. The Greek word does not denote an actual direction for the action of the verb.

†Paradise is the pleasant section of Hades under the earth. See footnote * on page 14.

References

[1] Jn. 11:25; 14:6; Col. 3:4
[2] 2 Pet. 1:4
[3] 1 Cor. 12:7; Eph. 4:7
[4] Matt. 25:14-30
[5] Eph. 2:18
[6] Acts. 10:34
[7] Matt. 1:20
[8] SS. 1:9
[9] SS. 3:4
[10] Heb. 4:14
[11] Col. 3:4
[12] Phil. 3:21
[13] 2 Cor. 12:2
[14] Phil. 3:11, 14
[15] 1 Thes. 4:16
[16] 1 Cor. 1:30
[17] Eph. 2:5
[18] Eph. 2:6
[19] Eph. 2:6
[20] Lk. 12:34
[21] Matt. 6:24
[22] Matt. 10:37
[23] Lk. 14:26
[24] Rev. 12:6
[25] 1 Cor. 3:2; Heb. 5:12-14
[26] Jn. 6:35; 1 Cor. 5:7-8
[27] Jn. 7:37-39; Rev. 22:17
[28] 2 Cor. 3:17
[29] 1 Cor. 3:1
[30] Eph. 4:13

CHAPTER 5

The State of Being

We come to that pronoun – the one that led into this whole book. It is often the case that the right scriptural question is a key to unlock the door to a treasure room. On one hand, some questions are satanic. Remember the evil one's first words to Eve: "Hath God said?"[1] Satan used a question to seduce and corrupt man. But not every question is devilish in nature. Some questions are simply the expression of a seeking heart. And, the Lord told us that he who seeks will find, and to him who knocks, it will be opened.[2] A proper question is the seeking for a godly treasure and the knocking on the door of God's storeroom, asking the Lord, Open to me! And so it was with this pronoun. The right question brought a response from the divine Spirit, opening the door to this book.

The Great Voice

And I heard a great voice in heaven, saying, Now is come the salvation, and the power, and the kingdom of our God, and the authority of his Christ: for the accuser of our brethren is cast down, who accuseth them before our God day and night. (Rev. 12:10)

In Revelation 12 the manchild is caught up to the throne of God. The manchild is comprised of all the martyred believers from the entire New Testament age, from Stephen to the very last one of the Christian martyrs as the age is about to change from the Church to Israel. When these are caught up to God's throne, a war will ensue. Michael and his angels will battle Satan and his, and cast them from heaven to the earth.

Then a great voice in heaven will declare, "Now is come the kingdom of our God and the authority of His Christ, for the accuser of our brethren is cast down, who accuses them before our God day and night." With this triumphant cry the firstfruits at the throne will celebrate the rapture of the manchild and the casting down of Satan.

However, the voice says that Satan accuses *them* before God day and night. And here is the troubling pronoun – *them!* Satan accuses *them!* Why doesn't the voice say that Satan accuses *us* day and night?

The manchild is composed of Christian believers, just as the firstfruits are. Furthermore, every Christian is aware of Satan's accusation – we all have experienced his vile accusation to God concerning us. We may not have observed the scene in the heavens, but in spirit we have sensed that accusation.

And, at the time of the rapture of the manchild, Satan is still accusing these martyrs, pointing out their flaws, their errors, their sins, their discrepancies with God in an effort to thwart their rapture to the throne. But why isn't Satan also accusing the firstfruits who are there in the heavens? This goes to the very heart of the difference between the firstfruits and the harvest.

The Wonderful Christ

While he was yet speaking, behold, a bright cloud overshadowed them: and behold, a voice out of the cloud, saying, This is my beloved Son, in whom I am well pleased; hear ye him. (Matt. 17:5)

...they say unto him, Teacher, this woman hath been taken in adultery, in the very act. Now in the law Moses commanded us to stone such: what then sayest thou of her? (Jn. 8:4-5)

Show me the tribute money. (Matt. 22:19)

Of all the billions of human beings that have walked upon the face of the earth, no one compares to the Lord Jesus. There never has been one like Him. He is exquisite in every way. With Him there is an answer to every problem and an abundance for every need. His beauty is captivating; His splendor is awe-inspiring. He is peerless, sufficient in every way for every circumstance.

When the woman was caught in adultery[3] and brought to Jesus, and He was asked what should be done to her by the Pharisees, He simply stooped down and with His finger wrote on the ground. That was an extremely agitated mob surrounding Him, trying to find fault with Him, willing to kill the woman caught in adultery to accomplish their evil purpose. But the Lord Jesus was unperturbed by all that went on around Him – He simply stooped and wrote on the ground. When the Pharisees continued to badger Him, He stooped and wrote something more on the ground. This silenced every one of them. From the oldest to the youngest they slithered away, hiding from the light upon the kind of people that they were. The Lord most probably had written their sins with his finger for all to see.

The woman must have been terrified, thinking she was about to be stoned to death. However, without saying a single word Jesus had dispersed every one of her accusers. She and He were left alone. What kind of person could do such a thing?

The Lord then asked the woman: "Did no man condemn you?"

The woman responded, "No man, Lord."

The Lord then said, "Neither do I condemn you. Go your way; from henceforth sin no more."

The Lord first asked whether any man condemned her, and then went on to say that He, the Son of God, did not condemn her either. How gentle His touch. How kind and reassuring His words. How did this woman feel after He spoke? Can you imagine how much she loved Him?

And then He told her to go her way, but did not stop there. He also told her to sin no more. He did not pretend that she wasn't a sinner. He spoke the truth in love to this poor woman. And yet He spoke in a way neither to condemn her nor drive her away. He spoke a word of salvation to her.

Consider how much of this amazing Person is seen in this one brief instance: His wisdom, His calm, His boldness, His gentleness, His kindness, His mercy, His love, His truth. Who can count how many facets of this divine "Gem" shine in this one short incident!

Near the end of His human life on earth, shortly before His crucifixion, Jesus was tested by the many groups of Jews in Jerusalem – the Pharisees, the Sadducees, the Herodians, the lawyers.[4] The Pharisees with the Herodians were the first to come to Jesus, trying Him. No doubt they had spent much time scheming and plotting how they could trap Jesus and ensnare Him with their words. They had devised a plot that they thought was inescapable.

They came to Jesus in an obviously hostile and devilish spirit to try Him: "Is it lawful to give tribute to Caesar or not?" In their consideration, there was no good answer. Whatever Jesus answered would be wrong. This was their deviousness, their subtlety, the Satanic evil within them. If Jesus answered it was lawful, then the people would hate Him, for the people hated the oppression of the Romans. If Jesus answered it was not lawful, then the Pharisees could accuse Him to the Roman governors. This was a wonderful trap, at least in their minds. There was no escape. They had ensnared this troubling Jesus. As they sprung their trap, they must have rejoiced, having finally put this little man, Jesus, down. They considered themselves so intelligent, so smart, so wise, so high. They did not know with whom they were dealing!

The Lord Jesus, and He is truly Lord, commanded them, "Show Me the tribute money." By such a word the trappers were trapped! First, they were doing the bidding of the Lord. They thought to entrap Him, and yet He was commanding them: "Show Me the tribute money." In essence He was telling them, "You are not in command of this situation, I am. I am the Lord and no one can usurp the Lordship from Me. You do not command Me. I command you. Show Me the tribute money." Jesus is the Lord! Jesus is the King and the King of Kings. No man rules Him.

In addition, it was not Jesus who had the Roman money. It was the Pharisees — the Roman money was in their pockets. They were the ones who trafficked in the Roman script. They were the ones who had knowledge of the Roman money. They were the ones who were part of the Roman system of things. When the Lord Jesus asked them, "Whose is this image and superscription?", they answered "Caesar's." They knew! They were familiar with everything Roman. They were exposed as the collaborators in the Roman system. They did not know with whom they were dealing!

Consider: in this circumstance, what would you have said? How would you have tried to escape the trap of the treacherous Pharisees? How would you have responded to their question? From a source that the human mind simply cannot comprehend the Lord Jesus uttered these words: "Render therefore unto Caesar the things that are Caesar's; and unto God the things that are

God's." This word left the Pharisees dumbfounded and defeated. They could never overcome Jesus. They did not realize how foolish their attempt to do so was.

However, their challenge afforded the Lord the opportunity to speak truth and impart something of God. His words are full of light. The Pharisees had Caesar's money in their pockets. They should give it back to Caesar. More importantly, they had something belonging to God that they were withholding from Him. Their whole being – spirit, soul, and body – was God's. He created it. Yet, they had taken it from Him. They should give themselves to God, for they belonged to Him.

To this day this one simple sentence leaves us speechless. What logic could come up with such a response? What person could utter such a word? What kind of being could respond in such a way?

Only Jesus. *Only Jesus!* He is the King. He is majestic, unconquerable, triumphant, wise beyond measure, undefeated and undefeatable. Who is like this Jesus? What kind of Being is He? He is unimaginably marvelous.

Shall I go on? How many books could be written about this Person? According to the apostle[5] the world itself could not contain the books. This is the wonderful Person with whom we have to do.

As we examine the life and Person of Jesus, as we inspect all His actions and deeds throughout His time on earth, we can find no flaw. In everything He was perfect. In every word He uttered, He was flawless. We can find no error, no unrighteousness, no sin, no misstep, no omission, no unkindness, and on and on and on. Nothing in Him was amiss, awry, or improper. He is perfect. And not only is He perfect, He is the kind of perfect that matches God's standard. It is not simply that He has done nothing wrong, which is so often our focus. Rather, it is that in everything an abundance of love and goodness flowed out from Him to all who were around. At every time and in every place, God flowed out of this man Jesus to everyone about. This is God's perfection, and this is what we see in Jesus.

During his life Jesus was tempted,[6] contradicted,[7] despised,[8] hectored,[9] threatened,[10] and eventually murdered.[11] However, through all this He lived a flawless life. There was no imperfection in Him. In all things and at all times God was expressed through Him. Satan could find no fault in this Person. Satan could never bring an accusation against Jesus to God, because he had no ground to accuse. Satan had nothing in the Son of God.[12]

The Peak and Goal

Ye therefore shall be perfect, as your heavenly Father is perfect. (Matt. 5:48)

...even as he chose us in him before the foundation of the world, that we should be holy and without blemish before him in love... (Eph. 1:4)

...and they sing as it were a new song before the throne, and before the four living creatures and the elders: and no man could learn the song save the hundred and forty and four thousand, even they that had been purchased out of the earth. These are they that were not defiled with women; for they are virgins. These are they that follow the Lamb whithersoever he goeth. These were purchased from among men, to be the firstfruits unto God and unto the Lamb. And in their mouth was found no lie: they are without blemish. (Rev. 14:3-5)

    The reason Satan does not accuse the firstfruits to God is because he can't. He has nothing to accuse them of. They have grown in Christ to full maturity. The divine life within them has spread throughout their entire being; the divine nature has become their nature. All that Christ is has become theirs. Christ has been appropriated by them, woven into their nature, and become their experience and person. The perfection exhibited in the life of Jesus is now theirs. They are perfect even as their heavenly Father is. There is no flaw in them. They are without spot, without blemish, and there is no guile in their mouths. They have reached the peak of the Christian experience, the end of the course, the goal of our Christian lives.

    These firstfruits do not acquire this perfection by self-effort. It is not something to which they attain by a lifelong process of self-mastery, asceticism, or some other kind of self-perfecting discipline. It is not some kind of sinless perfection that they are able to somehow synthesize in their lives. Even if it were possible to attain such a state, it would be a perfect, sinless *shell* with no content. They would be sinlessly perfect, yet without God. All their actions, deeds and words would impart nothing. Their only expression would be that of a self-righteous person. This is *not* what the firstfruits are.

These are not seekers of sinless perfection — they are seekers of Christ. Rather than spend their lives attempting to improve themselves, the firstfruits leave everything to seek and gain Christ.[13] Their lives are ones in constant and intimate contact with the Lord Jesus. Day by day and even moment by moment they look to Him for their supply, guidance, enjoyment, enrichment, and even their very person. He is before their eyes and He is what they seek. They realize the incurably fallen and pitiful condition of their self and willingly abandon that self to the cross, that they may gain Christ. Christ becomes everything to them, even their entire universe. They live in Him, for Him, and unto Him.

They don't attempt to perfect themselves, but rather they allow Christ to be perfected in them. Christ becomes their perfection. Their substance is Christ and their expression is Christ. What comes forth from them in their deeds and words is God in Christ flowing out to man.

Through a lifelong experience close to Christ, what He is becomes theirs. They are changed within. The natural and fallen element of the old creation is replaced by Christ, by the new creation. Christ becomes them. Like the apostle before them, it is no longer they that live but Christ who lives in them.[14] They reach the high peak and goal of Christian salvation, the perfection of which the Lord spoke in Matthew, and that for which every Christian has been predestined — standing before the Father, holy and without blemish. What possible accusation could Satan bring against these!

They have attained the divine standard of perfection — Christ. This is something law-keeping could never produce. No matter how good one behaves according to the law, such behavior is still without content. It is in empty semblance of reality.

In Our Image

And God said, Let us make man in our image, after our likeness...
(Gen. 1:26)

When God created man, He created him in His image. God did this for an extremely important reason. A glove is made in the image of a hand so that it may contain the hand. That is the sole reason for its form. Similarly, God made man in His image for a singular reason – that man might contain God, that God might be man's substance and content.

For example, man has the capacity to love. However, this love is a human shell. It is without divine content. This love is merely human, limited in capacity, temporal in existence, fragile and breakable in substance. It was not meant to remain empty by its Creator. It was meant to contain the divine love, which is unlimited, eternal, and indestructible.

When we are first regenerated, God enters into our spirit as the divine life. From there He begins His work to remake us in Christ's image. We all have been damaged within, some of us quite extensively. Abuse, addiction, sorrow, failure, success, sin, and so many other things have left us broken and impaired psychologically. The divine life works to heal us within, and concurrently to transform us gradually into Christ's image. He changes us in a divinely "metabolic" way, replacing the element of the old creation with Himself, thus making us into a new creation. Slowly He becomes our content – the divine "hand" fills the human "glove." His love fills our transformed love; His kindness fills our kindness; His strength fills our strength.

After many years, when this process is complete, as the final step the divine life swallows up our mortality, changing our body to be like the Lord's. The result is a person sharing God's divine life and nature, having God as his content, shining God forth through a mysterious transfigured body. Yet somehow we still exist, enjoying and participating in this amazing divine work.

Dried Out

And I saw, and behold, a white cloud; and on the cloud I saw one sitting like unto a son of man, having on his head a golden crown, and in his hand a sharp sickle. And another angel came out from the temple, crying with a great voice to him that sat on the cloud, Send forth thy sickle, and reap: for the hour to reap is come; for the harvest of the earth is ripe. And he that sat on the cloud cast his sickle upon the earth; and the earth was reaped. And another angel came out from the temple which is in heaven, he also having a sharp sickle. And another angel came out from the altar, he that hath power over fire; and he called with a great voice to him that had the sharp sickle, saying, Send forth thy sharp sickle, and gather the clusters of the vine of the earth; for her grapes are fully ripe. And the angel cast his sickle into the earth, and gathered the vintage of the earth, and cast it into the winepress, the great winepress, of the wrath of God. (Rev. 14:14-19)

Let both grow together until the harvest: and in the time of the harvest I will say to the reapers, Gather up first the tares, and bind them in bundles to burn them; but gather the wheat into my barn. (Matt. 13:30)

As the end of this age nears, the firstfruits will attain a marvelous state of being – the divine and uplifted state of Christ. They will be filled with Christ and clothed in Him. Everything about them will have the fragrance of Jesus. They will be without spot, blemish, or any such thing. They will have no guile; no lie will be found in their mouths. They will match Christ fully. In the heavens they will be a sweet savor of Christ to the Father and a deep satisfaction to the Son as His counterpart.

What will the state of the majority of believers be when they are caught up? Will they be mature? Revelation 14 seems to indicate this, for an angel declares that the harvest of the earth – the believers – is *ripe*. Let us examine the Scripture closely in order to arrive at the correct understanding of the condition of the majority of believers.

At the end of Revelation 14 there are two harvests.[15] The first is of the believers, while the second is of the evil armies of the earth – the grapes of wrath. Of the second harvest the word tells us it is time to gather them for they are *ripe*. The Greek word translated "ripe" in Revelation 14:18 means ripen to maturity. There is no question about their fitness for the reaping that will take place at Armageddon. They will have matured in evil and darkness. At Armageddon they will be reaped by being slaughtered.

However, when describing the harvest of the believers the Scripture uses a completely different word to describe their state. That word is also translated "ripe" in verse 15, but it is not the same as the word as in verse 18. In verse 15 the Greek word actually means "dried out." It does *not* mean ripened to maturity. The reason scholars translated this Greek word into "ripe" was a lack of understanding. They did not realize that this harvest will *not* be fully mature, will *not* be ripe at the time it is harvested. It will only be dried out. Maturity will come later.

Furthermore, in Matthew when the Lord spoke of this event, He said to let the wheat and the tares grow together until harvest. He did not say to let them grow until ripe. The Lord was careful and precise in His speaking.

After having passed through a time of intense suffering in the tribulation during which all the amenities, luxuries, and enticements of the world have been eliminated, the believers will be dried out of all the worldly "water." In fact, this is one of the main reasons that time of suffering comes. Once they have been fully dried out, there is no longer a reason to leave them on the earth, so the Lord catches them up to the air to meet with Him.

There will certainly be some growth in the divine life during that time – they are in the wilderness being nourished. So, they will grow in Christ. However they will not reach maturity by the end of the tribulation, at least not in general. They will not have overcome the world. Rather, the world was removed from them. That is not overcoming; it is the hand of a merciful God saving the believers from the world that had enticed and seduced them.

The Judgment Seat

When they meet with the Lord all the believers will stand before His judgment seat and give an account of what they did while in their physical bodies.[16] Some will receive a reward during the millennium, while others will receive a punishment. However, all the Lord does, whether reward or punishment, will be for the maturity of the believers.

In Summary

The firstfruits are those who arrive at the consummation of God's process of salvation prior to the last three and a half years of this age. They reach the high standard of divine perfection by gaining Christ within. Christ becomes everything to them, even their very person – for them to live is Christ.[17] As a consequence the Lord has no need to leave them on the earth during the tribulation. When the Lord takes them. they will ascend with the Lord to the throne of God for the Father's satisfaction. They will be perfect, just as their heavenly Father is perfect. They will be just as He is, complete, without spot or blemish, matching the Son of God in every respect.

The majority of the believers, however, are entangled with the world. They have not gained enough of Christ. Their focus is on something other than Christ. When the endtime comes they will not be mature. As a consequence they will be left to pass through the great tribulation. During that time they will be dried out from all the worldly "water." At the very end of the age, they will be taken to meet with the Lord in the air where He will judge every believer to determine whether they should receive a reward or punishment during the millennium.

References

[1] Gen. 3:1
[2] Matt. 7:7
[3] Jn. 8:3-11
[4] Matt. 22:15-46
[5] Jn. 21:25
[6] Matt. 4:1-11
[7] E.g., Jn. 2:20; 8:57
[8] Matt. 9:34
[9] Matt. 12:38; Jn. 8:5-7
[10] Lk. 4:30
[11] Lk. 23:20-24
[12] Jn. 14:30
[13] Phil. 3:8
[14] Gal. 2:20
[15] Rev. 14:14-16; Rev. 14:17-20
[16] 2 Cor. 5:10
[17] Gal. 2:20

CHAPTER 6

The Eternal State

Many Christians believe that they will spend eternity in heaven, that heaven is their eternal destiny. While they cannot quite define what heaven is, they have a general understanding that it is a place where everything is perfect, there are no problems, there is no sickness or death, God and Jesus are there, and in particular for each and every believer there is a kind of mansion awaiting them. They understand that to go to heaven is a change of location: now they are here on earth, and one day they will be there in heaven. There will be a change of physical place.

Only God knows how many believers think this way. However, from my interactions with Christians over the years it seems to be a very high percentage. They believe that when they die they will go to heaven, and that they will spend eternity in that place. However, such an understanding is not according to the Bible.

Not As Thought

This understanding that the believers will spend eternity in a kind of wonderful place, a Nirvana or Elysium, is not supported by a careful study of the Scriptures. First, we believers are *not* going to a physical place. Part of our being — our body — is physical. And, we were raised in a physical environment. We have very strong physical senses and ties to the physical realm. We are accustomed and attuned to physicality. Much of our concept of how things are and work is shaped by the physical universe around us and by our experience of it.

However, God is not physical,[1] nor are the angels.[2] Even the man, Jesus, who is with God[3] has a body that can no longer be described as something merely physical. It can disappear and appear;[4] it can change appearance.[5] It is in some mysterious way a spiritual body. To think that the believers are going to a physical place where they will spend eternity is something according to *human* concepts. It is based upon human thought of space and time. We are *not* going to a physical location for eternity. That is neither our goal nor our eternal state.

Second, we are *not* going to a mansion somewhere in the heavens, which the Lord Jesus has prepared for us. We do not have a mansion in heaven awaiting us. The usual citation for this belief is John 14:2, where the Lord told the disciples that He was going to prepare a place for them, and that in His Father's house are many mansions.[6] This understanding has proliferated within Christianity until it is now almost ubiquitous. However, it is based upon a serious mistranslation of the Bible. The word that is translated "mansions" in the King James and American Standard versions of the Bible simply means abiding places or abodes. It does not mean a mansion, nor does it imply that. It simply means a dwelling place, a place to abide. This bad translation of the Bible has fueled a serious misconception for centuries. The proper translation declares that in the Father's house there are many abodes, many dwelling places.

Furthermore, while the Lord did say that He was going to prepare this abiding place for us, in this same chapter of John He told us where He was going — He was going to the Father.[7] The Lord was speaking not of a physical place, but of a *Person*.

Finally we believers are not going to some kind of happy land in the sky. This concept is pagan in origin. It is seen in many pagan religions, such as in ancient Babylon, Egypt, and Rome, and even in modern Islam and Buddhism. It is absolutely not according to the Bible, nor is it a truly Christian belief.

A Person

In my Father's house are many mansions; if it were not so, I would have told you; for I go to prepare a place for you. And if I go and prepare a place for you, I come again, and will receive you unto myself; that where I am, there ye may be also. And whither I go, ye know the way. Thomas saith unto him, Lord, we know not whither thou goest; how know we the way? Jesus saith unto him,

I am the way, and the truth, and the life: no one cometh unto the Father, but by me. (Jn. 14:2-6)

Believest thou not that I am in the Father, and the Father in me? (Jn. 14:10)

...I go unto the Father. (Jn. 14:12)

The eternal God is thy dwelling-place, and underneath are the everlasting arms. (Deut. 33:27)

Lord, thou hast been our dwelling-place in all generations. (Ps. 99:1)

Yes, we are going, but not to a *physical* place. We Christians are going to a Person. Our destiny is God Himself. In John 14 the Lord speaks of the Father's house. When we hear this, our human minds immediately conjure up a kind of great physical dwelling. However, we should understand that the Father's house, of which Jesus spoke, is the Father Himself *as* the house. The Father *is* the house. The house of the Father is the Father as a house. We are going to a Person. The Lord told us this; however these words are largely overlooked or not understood.

The Lord told us He was going to the Father. He told us He was going in order that we might be where He is. But, He also said that He is in the Father. We are being brought into God in our experience. This is our dwelling place, our abode. *God* is our dwelling place! He dwells in us and we dwell in Him. We are not travelling to a physical location. We are travelling to God in Christ. This is our goal and our eternal state.

In John 14 the Lord said that He was going to prepare a place for us. He went on to say that He was going to the Father. He was going through death and resurrection, and by these accomplishments He was opening the way for man to enter into God. The way to God was closed in Genesis.[8] When man fell and sin entered into man,[9] the way into God was shut. By Christ's death and resurrection that door was reopened. His death took care of the problem of sin and His resurrection was proof of God's acceptance of that atonement. In His death the veil separating man from God was rent in two.[10] This was His preparation of a place for us in the Father. Man can now freely approach God in Christ. *That* is our eternal state.

Recall the Lord's last prayer while He was on the earth. In that prayer the Lord asked the Father, "That they may be in Us."[11] The Lord was beseeching the Father to bring the believers into God, for this is their eternal destination. It is not a physical place; it is a Person, the divine Person Himself.

A Change of State

...even as he chose us in him before the foundation of the world, that we should be holy and without blemish before him in love... (Eph. 1:4)

After these things I saw, and behold, a great multitude, which no man could number, out of every nation and of all tribes and peoples and tongues, standing before the throne and before the Lamb, arrayed in white robes, and palms in their hands; and they cry with a great voice, saying, Salvation unto our God who sitteth on the throne, and unto the Lamb. (Rev. 7:9-10)

Our eternal state is before the throne of God and in God. We are going to and into the Person of God. Our eternal state is not a change of physical position. It is altogether a change of our state of being. We are going from the physical and soulish to the spiritual. We are changing from temporal to eternal. Our experience, viewpoint, tastes, and everything about us is changing from earthly to heavenly. We are traveling from human to divine, from humanity to divinity. Our experience is changing from that of ourselves to God in Christ. Our whole state of being is changing. It is not a change of physical position. That is too low, too simplistic, too earthbound and dependent upon the physical universe. Our change is from everything to God Himself.

This change is accomplished very slowly. It happens day by day, in very small and often imperceptible increments. Bit by bit we are changed. In our long journey we pass from glory to glory,[12] from one stage of this change to another. Each "plateau" along this long upward climb is more glorious than the one before.

This takes place gradually. The Lord does this so that we do not get "lost" along the way. We are most precious to Him; He would not lose any of us. So He brings us step-by-step to our final resting spot, our dwelling in God, a bit at a time, in order to

Every One

...I give unto them eternal life; and they shall never perish, and no one shall snatch them out of my hand. My Father, who hath given them unto me, is greater than all; and no one is able to snatch them out of the Father's hand. (Jn. 10:28-29)

For I am persuaded, that neither death, nor life, nor angels, nor principalities, nor things present, nor things to come, nor powers, nor height, nor depth, nor any other creature, shall be able to separate us from the love of God, which is in Christ Jesus our Lord. (Rom. 8:38-39)

Not a single Christian will be lost in this long trek! We are held by two hands, the Lord's hand and the hand of the Father, who is greater than all. Furthermore, we are assured that nothing can separate us from the love of God in Christ. No matter what happens to us, what we pass through, what our present condition is, our eternal state is assured. Every Christian will be brought to that "spot," that state of being in the Father. Not a single one will be lost. God is amazing. We can only marvel at how He accomplishes what is on His heart. However, although every believer will reach this eternal state, there are many different paths that we follow to get there.

The Path of the Firstfruits

And I saw, and behold, the Lamb standing on the mount Zion, and with him a hundred and forty and four thousand, having his name, and the name of his Father, written on their foreheads. And I heard a voice from heaven, as the voice of many waters, and as the voice of a great thunder: and the voice which I heard was as the voice of harpers harping with their harps: and they sing as it were a new song before the throne, and before the four living creatures and the elders: and no man could learn the song save the hundred and forty and four thousand, even they that had been purchased out of the earth. These are they that were not defiled with women; for they are virgins. These are they that follow the Lamb whithersoever he goeth. These were purchased from among men, to be the firstfruits unto God and unto the Lamb. And in their mouth was found no lie: they are without blemish. (Rev. 14:1-5)

Before the last three and a half years of this age, all the firstfruits will be taken to the throne of God, their eternal state. They will be the first among all the believers to reach this final goal. They will be brought into God's house — into God Himself — and into the full experience of their dwelling in God.

They overcome all things, including their own selves,[13] to attain that state and position. They count all things loss that they might gain Christ, just as the apostle did thousands of years ago.[14] They seek Christ, follow Him, love Him, and are loved by Him. They will be the first ones to reach the eternal state.

The path will end for all these firstfruits from throughout the entire church age — they complete their course. For the last three and a half years of this age and for the entire thousand years of the millennial kingdom, they will enjoy in full their eternal dwelling in God, their eternal tabernacle.

If we were to liken the believers' experience to school — and in a very real sense we are being schooled — then the firstfruits will graduate. And not only so, they will graduate with highest honors. They will gain Christ in full. That fullness of Christ within them *will be* their graduation. However, for the rest of the believers something more will still be needed.

Remedial Action

And I saw, and behold, a white cloud; and on the cloud I saw one sitting like unto a son of man, having on his head a golden crown, and in his hand a sharp sickle. And another angel came out from the temple, crying with a great voice to him that sat on the cloud, Send forth thy sickle, and reap: for the hour to reap is come; for the harvest of the earth is ripe. And he that sat on the cloud cast his sickle upon the earth; and the earth was reaped. (Rev. 14:14-16)

For this we say unto you by the word of the Lord, that we that are alive, that are left unto the coming of the Lord, shall in no wise precede them that are fallen asleep. For the Lord himself shall descend from heaven, with a shout, with the voice of the archangel, and with the trump of God: and the dead in Christ shall rise first; then we that are alive, that are left, shall together with them be caught up in the clouds, to meet the Lord in the air: and so shall we ever be with the Lord. (1 Thes. 4:15-17)

For we must all be made manifest before the judgment-seat of Christ; that each one may receive the things done in the body, according to what he hath done, whether it be good or bad. (2 Cor. 5:10)

    Then what about the majority of the believers? When all the dead Christians are resurrected and are caught up to the air together with those who remain alive to meet with the Lord, they will stand before the judgment seat of Christ to give account for the things they've done during their lives, whether good or bad. This will be the time when the Lord judges every believer, not regarding their eternal salvation for that is secured, but regarding their status during the millennial kingdom. The Lord will determine whether a reward or a punishment is merited for each believer. With the firstfruits there will be no problem, for they will have gained that for which they were gained.[15] They will enjoy Christ and rule with Him.

    The Lord will judge the remainder of the believers by what they did in their Christian lives upon the earth. Every believer is given the Spirit when they are born again. The Holy Spirit is deposited within the spirits of the believers at the time of their rebirth.[16] But what have they done since then? Have they gained more of that Spirit? Have they allowed that Spirit of Christ[17] to move, flow, and spread within them that they might gain more of Him? In the words of the Lord's parable in Matthew 25,[18] have they purchased more oil? Do they have oil in their vessels or only in their lamps? All believers have oil in their lamps. That is to have the Spirit in their spirits, which occurs when they are regenerated. But how many "purchase" more oil for their vessels — that is, in their souls? In other words, how many gain Christ?

    Furthermore, each one of us has been given at least one talent from the Lord, a gift that we are to use and increase for the Lord at His return.[19] At His judgment seat we all have to answer for what He has given us. Have we invested and thereby increased what He has given us? Or, have we hidden His gift? Have we let it atrophy from lack of use? Have we let others invest while we enjoy the world or sit in a pew? This is how the Lord will judge the believers.

Those who receive a reward will enter into the Lord's joy and the thousand-year wedding feast, and share in the Lord's reign during the millennium. However, those receiving a punishment will be cast into outer darkness.[20] Some will receive lashes — few or many in some cases.[21] Others will be "cut asunder."[22] Some will even be saved through fire.[23] These are the serious consequences of ignoring what God has imparted to us and devoting ourselves to something other than God.

But in either case, whether reward or punishment, more growth in the divine life will generally still be needed. The firstfruits will have attained the eternal state; most, if not all, of the remainder of the believers will require some remedial action. If we again employ the school metaphor, the firstfruits will have graduated; the other believers will not. Some will require completing another "course" or two during the millennial kingdom. However, they will do so with joy as they participate in the wedding feast and in the Lord's rule on the earth. There will yet be a bit more work for them.

There will be some, however, who dropped out of school entirely. For them it is not a matter of gaining another "credit" or two. They ignored their needed schooling entirely. They spent their lives in the world, in something other than Christ. These will require a thousand years of discipline, sometimes severe, to bring them through the lessons they ignored in their lives on earth.

The Spiritual Body

Behold, I tell you a mystery: We all shall not sleep, but we shall all be changed, in a moment, in the twinkling of an eye, at the last trump: for the trumpet shall sound, and the dead shall be raised incorruptible, and we shall be changed. For this corruptible must put on incorruption, and this mortal must put on immortality. But when this corruptible shall have put on incorruption, and this mortal shall have put on immortality, then shall come to pass the saying that is written, Death is swallowed up in victory. O death, where is thy victory? O death, where is thy sting? (1 Cor. 15:51-55)

    There is a common understanding among Christians that when the Lord returns He will resurrect the dead believers and change the bodies of the living believers into spiritual bodies. According to 1 Corinthians this is absolutely correct. However, this understanding includes the assumption that once this event happens everything will be wonderful, that there will no longer be any problems no matter how we have lived our lives. The tone of the apostle Paul's writing in 1 Corinthians might be used to justify this conclusion. After all, Paul does say that what is mortal must put on immortality and corruption must put on incorruption. This certainly sounds wonderful. He also says that death is swallowed up in victory. Isn't this word implying a wonderful state of existence?

    If the apostle's words in 1 Corinthians were the only verses talking about this event, *then* that understanding might be justified. However, there are other verses that tell us something more about that happening. We cannot isolate a few verses from the Bible and expect to have a proper understanding of them.

    There are quite a few verses that speak about what happens after the event described in 1 Corinthians. It is absolutely true that at the last trumpet the dead will be raised with spiritual bodies and all the living believers will have their natural bodies changed. But as good as that sounds, it does not mean everything is okay, that everything is wonderful. In fact, that is not the case.

Punishment After Resurrection

But if that servant shall say in his heart, My lord delayeth his coming; and shall begin to beat the menservants and the maidservants, and to eat and drink, and to be drunken; the lord of that servant shall come in a day when he expecteth not, and in an hour when he knoweth not, and shall cut him asunder, and appoint his portion with the unfaithful. And that servant, who knew his lord's will, and made not ready, nor did according to his will, shall be beaten with many stripes; but he that knew not, and did things worthy of stripes, shall be beaten with few stripes. And to whomsoever much is given, of him shall much be required: and to whom they commit much, of him will they ask the more. (Lk. 12:45-48)

If any man's work shall abide which he built thereon, he shall receive a reward. If any man's work shall be burned, he shall suffer loss: but he himself shall be saved; yet so as through fire. (1 Cor. 3:14-15)

Consider Luke 12. There the Lord warns His disciples about His coming: those who did not do His will, will be beaten with stripes — some few, some many. This is a clear and unambiguous warning to all the believers that even after resurrection and after our natural bodies are changed, there can still be problems with the Lord that require His discipline.

Look at 1 Corinthians. There Paul warns the believers that some may suffer a punishment. Yes, all will be saved, but some will be saved *through fire*. Although our bodies will be changed, that does not mean everything will be wonderful after that. The Lord's coming and our meeting with Him are not as simple as many think.

Our True Nature Revealed

I counsel thee to buy of me gold refined by fire, that thou mayest become rich; and white garments, that thou mayest clothe thyself, and that the shame of thy nakedness be not made manifest... (Rev. 3:18)

Behold, I come as a thief. Blessed is he that watcheth, and keepeth his garments, lest he walk naked, and they see his shame. (Rev. 16:15)

What, then, does it mean to have a spiritual body? What it is precisely, we do not know. However, there are some implications in the Bible. Our natural bodies are "opaque." What we really are — our heart, our soul, the things concealed within us — is hidden by our natural body. While our body may manifest our inward condition to a small degree, in many cases it seemingly reveals nothing at all of what we really are. Many people pretend to be a certain way when in fact they are completely different. That is because our natural body is like a veil covering our true inward being.

On the other hand, our spiritual bodies are apparently transparent. Our true inward condition is manifested through that body. Whatever was hidden within our natural bodies while we lived on the earth will be apparent to all when those bodies are changed.

In Revelation 3 the Lord warns the believers in Laodicea (and all the believers as well[24]) to "buy" white garments from the Lord that the shame of their nakedness not be manifested. In Revelation 16 the Lord warns the believers who are passing through the great tribulation to keep their garments so that they do not walk naked, revealing their shame to others.

The garments in these verses refer to Christ, the Christ within us being lived out and manifested. This Christ covers us. Without such a Person in our experience we will be exposed, naked. Our true condition apart from Christ will be seen. All the dark, worldly, and earthly things within us that are still remaining will be displayed to all. This indicates that the spiritual body does not act as a cover to hide our condition; rather, it discloses what we are.

In this age we can pretend and hide the truth. In the next age, when we are in spiritual bodies, all will be manifested. If we spend much time gaining Christ in this age, then when our bodies are changed that Christ will be revealed. It will be a time of joy.

However, if we spend our current lives participating in and enjoying the world, when our bodies are changed our true inward condition will be seen. We will then be greatly ashamed. If we give ourselves over to the world in this age, we will be a shame in the next. It does not matter to what part of the world we give ourselves. It could be business, fashion, finance, religion, sports, amusements, music, or any one of the numerous parts of the dark world. It does not matter. The result is the same. In the next age we will be ashamed as our love for the world is exhibited to all.

Our True Condition

Then shall the kingdom of heaven be likened unto ten virgins, who took their lamps, and went forth to meet the bridegroom. And five of them were foolish, and five were wise. For the foolish, when they took their lamps, took no oil with them: but the wise took oil in their vessels with their lamps. Now while the bridegroom tarried, they all slumbered and slept. But at midnight there is a cry, Behold, the bridegroom! Come ye forth to meet him. Then all those virgins arose, and trimmed their lamps. And the foolish said unto the wise, Give us of your oil; for our lamps are going out. (Matt. 25:1-8)

In Matthew there is the parable of the 10 virgins. Five are wise and five are foolish. However, both the wise and the foolish are believers. The wise enter into the wedding feast[25] and the foolish address Jesus as Lord.[26] Furthermore, these all slept and then arose together to meet the bridegroom. Their sleep refers to their having died.[27] Their arising from sleep refers to their resurrection from the dead. In that they all arise together *at the time* the bridegroom comes also means they must be believers. Only the believers are resurrected at Christ's coming;[28] the unbelievers are not resurrected until *after* the millennium.[29] So these must all be believers.

In resurrection the lamps of the wise shine, for they take oil in their vessels. This oil refers to the Holy Spirit.[30] For the believers to have oil in their vessels is to have the Spirit spread into their soul.[31] In other words, the wise virgins had gained Christ during their lives. In resurrection that Christ will be manifested through their spiritual bodies. Their true condition will be seen. They had gained more of Christ after they were first regenerated.

The foolish exclaim that their lamps are going out! They have no oil in their vessels. Their true condition also will be made known at that time through their spiritual bodies. All will see, including themselves, that they had not gained Christ. While they will have Him in their regenerated spirits (i.e., their "lamps"), they will be void of Him in their person, in their souls. In other words, they will have no "oil" of the Spirit within their souls to shine brightly out through their spiritual bodies. The spiritual body will manifest what we really are, whether good or bad.

While 1 Corinthians 15 speaks of the changing of our body from its natural state to the spiritual, this is not as is generally supposed. For some it will be a great joy. For those who have gained Christ during their lives, it will be a wonderful experience.

However, for those believers who have lived apart from Christ in the world, this will be a great shame, an embarrassment, and an exposure of their true condition.

The Need for Further Perfecting

Then all those virgins arose, and trimmed their lamps. (Matt. 25:7)

Among the believers there are a good number who correctly understand that some Christians will be taken before the tribulation while the remainder will be taken at its end. However, their understanding of the believers' status during the millennium and the Lord's ongoing work within them may not be complete or entirely accurate.

Many of these believe that once the believers enter the millennial kingdom everything is complete, and no further work is needed within them. They don't realize that even if a believer is blessed to enter the wedding feast,[32] that still does not necessarily mean that the Lord's work is complete. While the firstfruits will have finished their course, most, and perhaps all, of the remainder of Christians will need further work from the Lord to mature them, even if they are blessed to enter the kingdom.

In Matthew 25 all ten virgins — foolish and wise — rose together and *trimmed their lamps*. In resurrected bodies their true inward condition will be seen and recognized. With such an exposure and realization, all the virgins will trim their lamps. That is, they will begin dealing with that part of themselves that requires adjustment. This means that *all* the virgins, even the wise, realize that further work within them is needed *after* resurrection. Within them there will still be certain things that require growth in life and transformation. Resurrection will not cure their inward shortages; rather, resurrection will reveal their lack and immaturity. Even the wise virgins, who enter the wedding feast, will see their need for further adjustment after resurrection.

Maimed, Halt, Blind

And if thy hand cause thee to stumble, cut it off: it is good for thee to enter into life maimed, rather than having thy two hands to go into hell, into the unquenchable fire. And if thy foot cause thee to stumble, cut it off: it is good for thee to enter into life halt, rather than having thy two feet to be cast into hell. And if thine eye cause thee to stumble, cast it out: it is good for thee to enter into the kingdom of God with one eye, rather than having two eyes to be cast into hell... (Mk. 9:43-47)

In Mark 9 the Lord says that if your eye causes you to stumble, cast it out. It is better for you to enter into the kingdom of God with one eye, than with both eyes to be cast into hell.* If your hand offends you, cut it off. It is better to enter into life maimed, than with two hands to go into unquenchable fire.

Of course the Lord was not talking literally. He was not speaking about the physical eye or the physical hand. We may pluck out our physical eye or cut off our physical hand, and then find that the inward problem causing our offense remains. The Lord was talking about our inward "eye," "hand," and "foot." He meant we should cut off whatever it is within us that causes us to stumble, in order that we might enter into life. It is better to enter the kingdom without what we cut off, than to be cast into fire with it during the millennium.

To enter into life is to receive the reward during the millennium. It is certainly not a punishment. However, according to these verses, some will enter into life blind in one eye or lame. They will enter the kingdom, but with a kind of "disability."

But in eternity every believer is without spot, without blemish, perfect, complete.[33] Therefore, during the millennium these who are disabled in some way will be healed, fully restored, and mature, having overcome that which was causing them to stumble.

These believers won't appear before the Father in an imperfect condition. Nor will they remain in such a condition for eternity. Rather, the millennium will be the time for them to be

---

* The Greek word translated "hell" actually means "Gehenna" or "Valley of Hinnom," which was a valley that surrounded Jerusalem's old city on the west and south. It was a place where idol sacrifices were offered, and it was considered accursed. Over time this name became synonymous with hell. However, in this context it does not mean that a believer will suffer eternal perdition. Rather, it means a believer might be "saved through fire" as mentioned in 1 Corinthians 3:15.

fully recovered. They will enjoy life and enjoy the wedding feast, but they will not yet be fully perfected.

Consider the Christian who suffers from an addiction of some sort or another due to a character flaw. Try as he might, this one cannot find the way to overcome that weakness in his personality. Rather than give into his addiction, indulge it, and be forced to deal with it "through fire"[34] in the millennium, he cuts it off. That is, he cuts off all opportunity for that addiction to usurp him, rule in him, and control him. He cuts off that whole realm of temptation. His weakness remains. He has simply cut off the opportunity for that weakness to destroy him. When this one enters into life in the millennium that weakness will still be with him, even though he has entered into life. During the millennium he will be helped to overcome that character flaw by experiencing the Christ who overcomes that weakness and heals him of his character flaw.

So then, some choose to cut off some part of themselves from functioning in order to enter into life. This is the much better choice. It is far better than letting the addiction continue to usurp and damage, and having to deal with that damage through fire in the next age.

Adjusted in the Wedding Feast

When thou art bidden of any man to a marriage feast, sit not down in the chief seat; lest haply a more honorable man than thou be bidden of him, and he that bade thee and him shall come and say to thee, Give this man place; and then thou shalt begin with shame to take the lowest place. But when thou art bidden, go and sit down in the lowest place; that when he that hath bidden thee cometh, he may say to thee, Friend, go up higher: then shalt thou have glory in the presence of all that sit at meat with thee. (Lk. 14:8-10)

In Luke 14 the Lord tells the disciples that whenever they are invited to a wedding feast they should take the lowest seats first. For if they take a chief seat, the master of the feast may come and tell them to make a way for someone more honorable than they.

That the Lord used the phrase "marriage feast" as opposed to simply the word "feast" indicates that He was particularly talking about that wedding feast during the coming millennium. Had He simply spoken of a feast, then we might consider that He was giving a general word to deal with our pride. By adding the word "wedding" He seems not only to be dealing with pride in general, but also addressing a specific situation that might occur at the beginning of the millennium.

For decades I simply could not understand how this could be. Wasn't everybody in the wedding feast fully transformed and mature? Weren't all character problems fully dealt with already in all those in the wedding feast? It was inconceivable to me that those in the kingdom at the wedding feast with the Lord Jesus would be so high-minded, brazen, and presumptuous.

However, knowing now that there is still much work to be done within the believers during the millennial kingdom, these verses make perfect sense. Some things in our nature take a very long time and an extended period of closeness with the Lord to eradicate. Some things, such as pride, are deeply entrenched within us. So it is certainly possible that some remnant of that pride remains in some believers during the millennium, and needs the Lord's direct touch to finally dispose of it altogether.

To the ones who think too highly of themselves, the Lord will tell them to make way for someone more honorable. To have such a word spoken in front of all the believers at the wedding feast is indeed a great shame. It will certainly be a serious blow to the pride of those who are presumptuous, the effects of which will endure for the rest of the millennium.

Eternal Tabernacles

And I say unto you, Make to yourselves friends by means of the mammon of unrighteousness; that, when it shall fail, they may receive you into the eternal tabernacles. (Lk. 16:9)

In Luke 16 the Lord speaks an enigmatic parable. The Lord commends an unrighteous steward for his actions in helping others, even though he did it unrighteously. He then goes on to say we should make friends with the mammon of unrighteousness, that when it fails they may receive us into the eternal tabernacles. To what does this parable refer?

There are questions about this word that require answers. Who was the one making friends with the mammon of unrighteousness? And, what are the eternal tabernacles? And who are the "they" that are receiving others into those tabernacles? Without answers to these questions, it's impossible to understand the Lord's speaking.

First, this word has nothing to do with the unbelievers. The Lord was speaking to His disciples when He said that they should make friends with the mammon of unrighteousness. This is a word for the believers, and consequently those who are to make friends with the mammon of unrighteousness are believers.

Next, who are the "they" that are receiving others into the eternal tabernacles? They must also be believers. Who would be in eternal tabernacles other than Christians? So then, some believers are receiving other believers into eternal tabernacles.

These verses speak of some believers welcoming others into their eternal tabernacle or dwelling place. When does this occur? It can't be before the endtime because the believers have not yet entered their eternal abodes by that time. In addition, it can't be after the millennium because all the believers will then be in their eternal abodes. Therefore, this must refer to something during the millennium.

But what are the eternal tabernacles? These verses can be explained in this way. Before the last three and a half years the firstfruits will enter into their eternal state in God, before the Father. That is their eternal dwelling place, or their eternal tabernacle. They will enjoy this wonderful state of being, this "place," until the end of the millennium. Then the remaining believers will join them.

However, during the millennium the majority of believers will be still be journeying toward to that state. At that time they can participate in the firstfruits' enjoyment, condition, status, and experience by being received into the firstfruits' abode or tabernacle. To be received into their abode is to enter into that same fellowship and communion that they have with the Father and the Son.

During their lives on the earth, some believers helped others financially or in some other practical way. That help will be remembered in the coming age by those who have already entered their eternal dwelling. In response to that help, they will have open and welcoming hearts toward those believers who helped them and who have not yet matured. These will be welcomed into the experience of the firstfruits, which is the fellowship they enjoy with the Father and the Son. In that fellowship the immature believers will grow and mature as well.

In Summary

The firstfruits will be fully mature before the last three and a half years of this age. During those last years they will enjoy the eternal state before the Father and with the Lord Jesus. Then, during the millennium they will reign with Christ.

The other believers need further work and spiritual growth to reach the final goal. Some will enter the wedding feast during the millennium and take part in the Lord's joy as they reign with Him. However, they will not yet be fully grown. They will still require some discipline, training, and growth in life during that time to reach the eternal state.

Others will be seriously stunted in their growth in the divine life. They will be very immature. They spent their lives in the world and loving something of the world. As a consequence they will spend that thousand years in outer darkness. They will be outside the glory of the kingdom. There they will weep and gnash their teeth[35] as they regret having spent their lives in the world, something that was temporal and passing away.

Some of these will be those who beat their Christian brothers.[36] They had such a high regard for themselves that they presumed to adjust others by psychologically beating, reproving, abasing, and debasing them, and at the same time exalting themselves. These will face a much more severe discipline during the kingdom,

For those believers outside of the glory of the kingdom there will be various disciplines and punishments. Some will be lashed with stripes, either few or many. Some will even be saved through fire. However, all of this will be God's way of bringing these immature and seriously malnourished believers to their final goal — the eternal state.

God is God — nothing can deter Him from His purpose. By the end of the millennial kingdom He will have brought every believer to full maturity. Then all will be before Him in love. It is for this that we have been predestined. There is no escaping this destiny!

Through various means God will mature every believer by the end of the millennium. Then they will both enjoy and *be* that New Jerusalem seen at the end of Revelation.[37] This is the eternal, spiritual abode of every believer. How amazing our God is! Praise him!

References

1. Jn. 4:24
2. Heb. 1:7
3. Acts 7:56
4. Jn. 20:26
5. Lk. 24:15-16
6. Jn. 14:2
7. Jn. 14:12
8. Gen. 3:24
9. Rom. 5:12
10. Matt. 27:51
11. Jn. 17:21
12. 2 Cor. 3:18
13. Lk. 14:26
14. Phil. 3:8
15. Phil. 3:12
16. Jn. 3:6; 1 Cor. 6:17
17. Phil. 1:19
18. Matt. 25:9
19. Matt. 25:14-30
20. Matt. 25:30
21. Lk. 12:47-48
22. Matt. 24:48-51
23. 1 Cor. 3:12-15
24. Rev. 3:22
25. Matt. 25:10
26. Matt. 25:11
27. Acts 7:60; 13:36
28. 1 Thes. 4:16
29. Rev. 20:5
30. Acts 10:38
31. 2 Cor. 4:7
32. Rev. 19:9
33. Eph. 1:4; 5:27; Matt. 5:48
34. 1 Cor. 3:15
35. Matt. 22:13; 24:51; 25:30
36. Matt. 24:48-50
37. Rev. 21-22

APPENDIX

The Manchild

The manchild is a special and extraordinary case. He is comprised of all the New Testament martyrs, of all those who have been killed for the Lord during the entire church age. Some of these, like the apostle Paul, fully matured and reached the goal. It is apparent that many did not, for Satan will still be accusing them at God's throne.[1] They evidently still had some flaws, problems, and a lack of maturity at the time of their deaths.

These had their lives cut short by the evil one before they had the opportunity to mature. They gave up their lives for the Lord and in so doing gave up the chance to mature in Him during this age. They valued the Lord Himself more than themselves and more than their own spiritual maturity. How precious these are.

Not Forgotten

And when he opened the fifth seal, I saw underneath the altar the souls of them that had been slain for the word of God, and for the testimony which they held: and they cried with a great voice, saying, How long, O Master, the holy and true, dost thou not judge and avenge our blood on them that dwell on the earth? And there was given them to each one a white robe; and it was said unto them, that they should rest yet for a little time, until their fellow-servants also and their brethren, who should be killed even as they were, should have fulfilled their course. (Rev. 6:9-11)

God would not forget their sacrifice. How dear all these ones who laid down their lives are to Him. As their number is multiplied by the intense martyrdom that will come at the end of the age, all the martyrs under the earth will cry out to God, asking Him how long it will be before He avenges their blood upon those who dwell upon the earth.

In response they are all given a white robe. This robe is not only a sign of God's approval of these martyrs, but also Christ in a particular way. This robe qualifies them to appear before God after they are resurrected. It is Christ clothing and covering them, and in particular covering those aspects that are not yet fully up to the divine standard. Any spots or blemishes that remain will be covered by the Lord.

When the church age closes, their number will be completed. At that time the Lord will catch* them up to the throne of God. They will be given the privilege of commanding the battle to cast Satan and his forces from before the throne of God and from the heavens to the earth. This will be a reward to them for their offering of themselves in love to the Lord by martyrdom.

In addition, it is their appearance before the throne of God that is the main factor in righteousness that initiates the casting out of Satan. God is righteous in all things. He would not cast out anyone, even Satan, unjustly. He treats even His great adversary righteously.

When the manchild arrives in the heavens, they will be the living proof of Satan's murderous misdeeds. God's righteous judgment for these killings, all of which were instigated by the evil one himself, will be the casting out of Satan from the heavens and from before the throne of God forever. God will give the martyred believers the right and authority to pronounce and enforce His judgment. The martyrs will then direct the godly angels to execute this judgment upon Satan.

They will then enjoy the last three and a half years of this age with the firstfruits on the heavenly Mount Zion. They will also participate in the millennial kingdom, partaking of the Lord's reign and of His joy while they grow to maturity. They will be given the opportunity that was taken from them when they were on the earth.

By the end of the millennium they too will be fully mature and will enter into the eternal state, their abode and eternal tabernacle in God. For eternity they will bear the divine mark of

---

*This is the same word that is used for the rapture of the majority of believers in 1 Thessalonians 4. Like them, the manchild will require an external force to catch them away from the earth.

those who died for Christ. As the apostle Paul said, "Henceforth let no man trouble me; for I bear branded on my body the marks of Jesus."[2] The mark of their martyrdom will be an eternal glory for these dear and precious ones who died for Christ.

References

[1] Rev. 12:10
[2] Gal. 6:17

BIBLIOGRAPHY

Strong, James. *Strong's Exhaustive Concordance of the Bible: Updated and Expanded Edition.* Hendrickson Publishers Marketing, LLC, 2007

Vincent, Marvin R. *Word Studies in the New Testament.* Grand Rapids: Wm. B. Eerdmans Publishing Co., 1977